AF413150

MISSING THE BUS

MISSING THE BUS

Basic Life Skills for the 21st Century: Solid Foundation of a Healthy, Prosperous and Meaningful Life

Neelesh M Kajale

Notion Press

Old No. 38, New No. 6
McNichols Road, Chetpet
Chennai - 600 031

First Published by Notion Press 2017
Copyright © Neelesh M Kajale 2017
All Rights Reserved.

Hardcase ISBN: 979-8-89519-211-5
Paperback ISBN: 978-1-94686-963-0

www.missingthebus.co.in
www.facebook.com/kajaleneelesh
neelesh@missingthebus.co.in

For Information about Special discounts available for bulk purchases, contact Neelesh at neelesh@missingthebus.co.in

DISCLAIMER

This book and the content provided herein are simply for self-help purpose. Every effort has been made to ensure that the content provided in this book is accurate and helpful for our readers at the time pf publishing. However, this is not an exhaustive treatment of the subjects. No liability is assumed for losses or damages due to the information provided. Readers are responsible for their own choices, actions and results.

I would like to dedicate this book to my father,
my grandmother & my mama.
I owe you everything.

TABLE OF CONTENTS

PREFACE

It was a long day... I was returning home after meeting old friend of mine who was leaving for USA on a new assignment. We had an intriguing discussion about the importance of keeping ourselves updated about the new technologies and innovations related to workplace and personal lives. The discussion was mainly about how critical it is to keep our skillsets in sync with the changing professional and personal lives. We can take advantage of all the technological advancements only if we are ready with relevant tools and modern day weapons of knowledge and their application in daily routine.

Let me introduce myself first, I am a constant learner. Learning various new things as I go along is my favorite hobby. It has been a fantastic journey so far..

I have had the privilege of being born and brought up in a beautiful and picturesque town of Satara Maharashtra. My parents are teachers. The importance of being a good human being above anything else was inculcated on our minds from very early days of our lives. My parents had a typical Indian approach to money, health and food. On the weekends, we used to walk 4-5 kilometers from the market to our home near Mahabaleshwar when I was 7-8 years old. My father used to discuss various things with us as we walked towards our home. The topics used to be very random. These little discussions and his interesting stories had a very deep influence on my life. He always insisted on being polite and sincere. He taught us never to judge others by their appearance or behavior.

Those early sessions of grounding had a very sobering effect on my attitude and behavior towards people and situations I got involved with in my life.

I was lucky enough to have spent my childhood in an excellent atmosphere of Satara. Satara is a small town near Pune Maharashtra, it has a fascinating tradition and history of being at the forefront of Freedom Struggles. We were extremely lucky to have a chance of learning from the people/teachers/guides, who had dedicated their lives towards those specific subjects or knowledge streams. Academic competition was so strong in our classrooms. We had some of the most intelligent students and proficient teachers navigating the future course of academic excellence.

This academic talent had a flip side too. Typically the academic excellence of 10% students puts remaining 90% students under tremendous pressure to study and perform. Some of them manage to cope up with the pressure and come out with the flying colors, while remaining students get their self-esteem and confidence scarred for life with inferiority complex. Thankfully, we could manage to survive the onslaught of brilliant students who used to achieve 98% marks always and every time. In the process, we ended up reaching 80%-85% bracket ourselves. This is a typical positive peer pressure scenario, if handled correctly.

Besides excellent educational facilities, we also had a well formed sports culture. We used to spend a lot of time playing outdoor sports like Cricket, Football with our close friends. These experiences have certainly helped us becoming better team players and individual performers.

We were fortunate to have spent our childhood in a very healthy natural surroundings. The atmosphere we grew up in is one of the best in the region. Beautiful, natural non-polluted surroundings play very important part in overall development of an individual. This nourishing environmental/social/academic climate grooms an individual and helps form intellectual, health related and social habits and behaviors.

After eventful schooling, I had left for Pune to complete engineering and subsequently to Bengaluru for a job in the IT field. After spending some years in Bengaluru in IT technical presales division, I requested our company HR head for internal transfer to Mumbai in Sales department. That was the most challenging and fulfilling decision of my life. Being very aware of the fact that I am not a Sales material by character, I pushed myself to get out of my cocoon and learn some very important skills of Business Communication, time management and social skills.

Mumbai being a Melting pot of various cultures and mindsets, it makes everybody learn to survive and adapt to difficult situations and scenarios. The pace of personal growth in Mumbai can be staggering if taken in a right way. The extreme pressure of city life, work commute, work related pressure and lack of time spent in pure interpersonal relationships can take a toll if not handled properly.

Spending first 20 years of life in blissful and nourishing environment, next 4 years in Bengaluru witnessing the Start Up of Indian Silicon Valley, subsequent 12 years in the rumble of Financial capital of India prepared myself to take some challenging decisions of leaving the corporate life and start on my own in Hospitality and other entrepreneurial projects.

After experiencing sweat/bitter tastes of the entrepreneurial adventures and a near fatal health scare, I had to sit back and take a balanced view of the situation. Fortunately, this forced break gave me an opportunity of spending some time evaluating my journey so far, reviewing my original goals/objectives, restructuring my priorities and making necessary changes/arrangements towards achieving the revised goals.

While reevaluating all the personal, professional and financial decisions i had taken throughout my life, I can very clearly see some glaring aspects missing from the learning process. I can very candidly conclude that, most of the struggle/frustration I have gone through in my adult life is not because of professional incompetence or lack of technical/operational knowhow of domains related to my profession but due to my complete lack of understanding of life skills/soft skills, financial literacy and health aspects.

As I had mentioned earlier, I had an excellent academic and professional (Engineering) training. I can very confidently conclude that the things which are affecting our personal growth is lack of awareness and education of Life soft skills, Financial literacy and most importantly Health literacy. Most of my professional life could have been a very different story, if I had studied these critical aspects of Financial Literacy, Health Literacy and Soft Skills early in the life.

I am not trying to blame our Educational institutes or our teachers or parents or Government machinery for this lack of awareness. I am sure they are taking all the steps necessary from their side to alleviate these glaring roadblocks on the Success Expressway.

We, all of us in our own capacity, must make sure that these illiteracy issues related to Personal Health, Finance and life skills are taken care of. We must take every possible action to educate ourselves, our children, our colleagues and our society about these basic aspects of life.

If we fail to take any action on these illiteracy issues immediately, we may end up paying a very heavy price in terms of wasting our precious resources like Intelligence, Time, Health and above all peace of mind. Lack of understanding of these basic aspects of demanding 21st Century Life, will expose us to a very big challenge from the local/global competition and we'll end up wasting most of our adult life correcting these stupid mistakes instead of focusing on building our lives based on our academic/professional competence.

It gives me immense pleasure in presenting to you my understanding of these aspects so that we can learn, re-learn and be ready for the demanding careers and fulfilling lives.

Let us not "Miss the Bus".

Neelesh Kajale

www.missingthebus.co.in

Mumbai, INDIA

28th Feb 2017

ACKNOWLEDGEMENTS

I am grateful to a lot of people who have motivated and inspired me to write. I would like to thank my family members especially my mother, my wife and my cute children Sharvari & Ojas for their continuous & unwavering support and understanding.

Without the significant contributions made by all of my wonderful classmates in schools and colleges, my energetic colleagues in various organizations, it would not have been possible to learn so many things and to be able to put it in the form of this book.

I would like to express heartfelt gratitude to my dear friends and schoolmates Mr. Pramod Vitthal Shinde & Mr. Santosh Arvind Kadam for their amazing support and inspiration at the start of my eventful journey in Bengaluru.

CHAPTER 1

WHY THIS BOOK?

We have very robust academic institutes and learning infrastructure. We have been at the forefront of academic excellence in India and abroad. Our professional competence and attitudes are very well appreciated and awarded across the globe. We have a very well-oiled machinery in place for producing highly qualified and efficient resources, who can compete with the best in the world.

Though there is a certain scope of improvement in the academic setup, we need to focus on a far bigger issue at hand. We are not giving enough attention and importance to empowering our children and youth with basic life skills and awareness about their personal finance and health. Lack of these basic skills are putting enormous pressure on our children, youngsters and adults. Lack of skills awareness is hampering the growth of the individuals and society. We are not being able to take advantage of our full potential since we are spending significant amount of time and resources in committing and correcting avoidable mistakes.

It is of paramount importance to understand the issue and take necessary actions immediately.

Let us start with understanding the situation first:

Life skills can be defined as the skills necessary to face everyday life situations and challenges effectively. These situations can be faced everywhere like at school, at social events/gatherings, on the sports grounds, in our personal lives, at our office etc. Individuals who are able to understand and learn these skills and effectively utilize these skills along with their educational qualifications will be better placed to utilize most of the educational and employment opportunities. Understanding of these skills will give them added advantage by helping take right decisions and actions at the right time.

The cumulative effect life skills can have on an individual and our society can be huge, bringing positive changes in the employability and efficiency of the working class. Learning life skills is an unavoidable part of being able to meet the challenges of everyday life. The changes in local and global economies and social aspects over the last few years are because of immense progress made in the field of Technology. The advent of modern technology is transforming our society, workplace and home. To survive these changes in the modern life, we must learn new skills which will match with the performance requirements of the modern society and workplace.

The nature of the job requirements and associated skill sets are changing at a very fast rate. We need to be flexible and ready to adapt to the situation without losing precious time.

Individuals can get benefitted from developing these life skills. We will be able to find new ways of finding solutions to teething issues and will be able to approach problems from different perspectives. We will be able to recognize the impact of our actions. We will be ready to take the responsibility of our actions instead of looking for scapegoats. We will be confident in communicating, co-operating with peers or different groups effectively. We will be ready to analyze multiple options, make informed decisions and evaluate multiple choices available to us before they are implemented. We'll be able to appreciate others while being aware of our own strengths and weaknesses.

While we work hard to excel in academics, most of us find it difficult to get a job. Biggest gap is between expectations of the employee and the employer. The mismatch is between the skills which the employer is looking for in his potential employee and the skillsets, a potential candidate possesses.

Understanding of the soft skills helps us work as a part of a team, it helps us understand business processes, solve problems, time and people management. It helps us adapt to different roles and positions. It helps us get leadership opportunities by showcasing our strengths and talent.

If all of us can work on improving life skills, collective impact on the society can be monumental. As we keep on working on improvement in our life skills, the society will get benefitted immensely. It helps us raise our awareness about other cultures and improve our global outlook. It makes us respect diversity of thoughts, customs and cultures. It allows us to come together in developing a more inclusive and tolerant society. It helps us navigate different difficult situations by negotiating tactfully with them resulting into resolution of differences of opinions and mutually beneficial agreements.

Out of syllabus?

When I was interviewed for different roles in my career, one very common selection parameter was "Communication Skills". Can we think about any instance wherein we were taught about basic life skills in our schools or colleges? There is a possibility of one or more cursory happenstances but largely these topics were never part of the syllabus until later years in Engineering. By the time, I had studied communication skills as part of the academic syllabus, my communication patterns were already set based on the environment in which I had grown up. I had developed my style of communication by observing different people and their ways of communication, Or by watching a lot of Hollywood movies for that matter. The things I had learnt about communication had neither scientific base nor were they primed for employability.

As we make progress in our chosen profession, we end up communicating with so many people almost every day. Individuals who are working in various industries after graduating from different colleges in various streams must be facing the challenges related to effective communication.

If we study Employability reports in different industries, we can observe a very common gap in the skill sets they are looking for in the candidates i.e. communication skill. Communication skill is very important skill in social, personal or corporate environment. It helps us exchange views, ideas with others effectively. It helps us avoid and resolve conflicts or differences of opinions constructively by discussing the issues. In my personal opinion, being a good listener is one of the most underrated communication skill. Active listening is a very essential aspect of communication because it helps us express solidarity with others, it helps us resolve conflicts without name calling. Imagine if conflict avoidance and resolution by proper communication can be taught to all the students very early in their lives, don't you agree that a lot of unnecessary and unpleasant situations can be avoided in one's personal or professional life?

Learning a new skill is easy when we are young, whether it's learning a flute or a Guitar or learning a new language. It helps us save a lot of struggle later in our life. In India, we have 35 major languages and various dialects. Due to rapid industrialization, we are getting an opportunity of working with people from different backgrounds, speaking different dialects. English being a common global language, is helping us communicate with most of the people. Changing global scenarios will certainly push us towards an opportunity of working with people of different nationalities and languages. In such a scenario, effective communication skill is going to be a very important tool of personal success.

We are discussing about educating children and adults alike about basic life skills right from the start of their schooling, we need to focus on different life skills immediately. These skills are Finance skills, Health awareness and Food awareness besides other soft skills like time management etc.

We are very strong on the academic education front covering subjects like Science, Math, and History etc. Considering the probability of using this knowledge in day to day life, we can very safely say that most of the knowledge acquired is used very rarely based on nature of our job. But how often do we communicate with people? How often do we take personal financial decisions? How often do we take proactive steps at maintaining or improving our health? How selective are we about our food from health perspective? Considering the frequency of utilization of these activities, we must immediately start focusing on educating ourselves and our children about these basic life skills.

I think, it is safely assumed that these basic skills are learnt by children at their homes and schools by observing others in their vicinity, which they will learn themselves as they grow up, that these skills anyways are easy skills and we don't have to pay extra attention towards them. Unfortunately, these assumptions are plain wrong and the child or an adult ends up paying up for these assumptions throughout his/her life.

Mandatory life skill education

Education by definition is the act or process of acquiring knowledge or information or understanding or skills from somebody or something. It is expected to prepare us for the future. The future which involves taking all steps necessary for achieving success by the parameters set by the society and our culture. The most important aspect of education is to prepare a student for becoming a worthy citizen of the society, who can take care of the wellbeing of himself, his family and in turn can contribute to the larger good of the society. It necessarily means that we are earning our livelihood by applying our skillsets which in turn are contributing to the development of our society. Different roles which can help us achieve these results are farmers, teachers, engineers, doctors, government employees, entrepreneurs etc.

There is often a mismatch between what we are learning in the classroom and the expectation from us out of the classroom. Let us consider our job market. It is a very common observation made by the industry leaders that Employability of the candidates is declining. Candidates are getting educated for employment, they are not getting educated for the employability. Only two out of ten employers think that all or most educated candidates are "EMPLOYABLE". Vast majority of employers say that the educated candidates lack key employability skills such as communication skills, teamwork, and ability to work under pressure. Result of this skills gap is customer dissatisfaction and loss of business. In short, if the purpose of education is to prepare individuals for the employability, it seems we're not achieving the results due to whatever reasons. Technical competence is extremely important but that can be applied only if the candidate reaches the stage of employability cycle wherein his technical acumen can be tested. Most of the candidates are failing in the basic parameter of gaining employability itself.

Typically we are teaching languages with their grammar and vocabulary to the students, making them pass one exam after the other in schools. This process is happening without teaching the students about taking practical advantage of these language skills in day to day life.

The speed at which national/global employment scenarios are changing is putting all of us in the grave danger of finding ourselves outdated and outplaced in the workplace of the future. If the current education is not being able to cover some of the aspects of the skills gap, how can we work towards making them ready for facing the challenges of the future?

In a typical day in the life of a successful corporate employee, what kind of activities he has to complete? What skillsets does he uses to accomplish results from these activities? We keep our clients updated by communication with them over the phone or by email. We attend meetings with our colleagues. We discuss various solutions and issues with each other. We understand the problems clients are facing. We keep our management informed about the feedback we are getting from the clients. We help our clients solve their issues by proposing most suitable and cost effective solution. We follow up with our various company departments about project execution and payment collections. We design solutions for the clients after understanding their requirements. We write software programs after requirement gathering and need analysis etc. We organize our time schedules, we prioritize our tasks, we delegate some of the work to our peers and so on, we manage work related stress, we manage commute exertion etc... We end up repeating various tasks mentioned above in our personal, social lives. These are the soft skills we are taking advantage of in furthering our well-being and growth. We are doing most of these activities without consciously trying to improve their effectiveness. These are the skillsets we should be really focusing on along with the technical and academic excellence.

What we are actually doing while performing above mentioned tasks is using various soft skills like communication skills, persuasion skills, presentation skills, time management, problem solving, team building, stress management all the while taking care of our health and finances.

Workplaces today is a mix of team members from various cultures and backgrounds with their set belief systems and thought processes. Important aspect about the communication between such a team members is expressing our views in a common language like English in such a way that nobody gets confused or hurt or offended. To achieve this level of proficiency in communication, we must make conscious efforts to hone our language skills especially if the common language in question is not your mother tongue or first language.

Are we missing something?

We are teaching our students to memorize their syllabi and clear exams with flying colors. This is certainly helping us to a limited extent and we are surviving with these tactics till now. We are ignoring the critical life skills by assuming that parents will take care of coaching their kids on the critical life skills such as communication, finance management, time management and so on. This is a complex situation. Unfortunately even educated parents are not trained with these skills. Some of the parents are not qualified enough to teach these lessons while most of the parents assume that school learning is enough for successful career and fruitful life. Considering the fact that, schools have the best and the biggest opportunity of teaching their students these skillsets. They have the infrastructure ready, they have the audience ready. The issue is the audience is not aware of their needs and when they become aware of the need for indispensable skillsets, it is already too late. Then we end up spending a lot of resources like time and money to acquire these skillsets later in the life.

We'll have to focus on educating students about personal finances, personal development, communication, Emotional Intelligence and healthy living. Schools will be the best place to inculcate these thought processes on the young impressionable minds, anything later than school years will not yield expected results since a lot of students drop out before the college. Important subjects or life skills that can be incorporated in the schools is Money Management, Interpersonal communication, Finance management, Time Management, Stress Management and Health awareness.

What extra things do we need for specialized jobs?

Education for employment and Education for Employability are two very different things. If the schools are supposed to educate students for Employment, they are falling behind substantially. The knowledge we get from the schools and new age skill sets required in the market are not in sync.

Just to mention, let me point out a fact that when a Software company in Pune hires a fresh graduate (Typically an Engineering graduate), he is made to undergo a 3 month or six month 'On The Job Training' about the work he is supposed to do. Of course a college cannot teach all the software methodologies and advanced technologies but the gap is visible. Schools and colleges are developing technical competence and content whereas training on the context in which this content is supposed to be used and the skillsets required for using the content in the right context are missing.

Let us consider a scenario A, I have got excellent qualifications for a job opportunity but am not conversant with the technology I am supposed to work on. I'll need to be trained for three months by the company. Whereas my friend has got similar qualifications and he knows the technology too. From company management perspective, my friend is the candidate who can be productive from the day one and hence gets selected. Morale of this scenario is my friend spent extra time and energy on learning new technology whereas I was waiting for a job based on my mere academic qualifications. On the similar lines, if I have additional technology certification along with academic qualification, I will be given a preference in selection for the job because company will not have to spend additional money and time on my certification.

Companies often prefer readymade material for their jobs, typical "Plug & Play" types. They would rather hire a candidate who had a proven record of doing the job against someone who has a paper that says he might be a good employee, after training.

We need to build skills and experience in our desired field. Let us not expect our college degree to land us a good job unless we have relevant work experience or training. Having the ability to learn a skill set will not help us when our competition already has that skill set.

Marking or grading system used in the school is misleading. In our school, we were always pushed to get above 90/100 marks in all the subjects all the time. (Many of us managed to get above 90/100 almost every time for 12 continuous years, while some of us including myself were comfortable getting 80/100 while being busy playing on the ground all these years).

Thankfully enough, there is sufficient space in life for 80/100 people with specialized skills.

Schools have a very predictable system of marks or grades. We can be certain about the fact that if we can take a certain amount of efforts in an organized and systematic way, we can be sure about getting a certain amount of marks or grades. Life cannot be so simple. Even after putting in certain efforts in the most organized and disciplined manner, we can never be sure about getting "A" most of the time. Schools train us to expect predictable results after known efforts whereas life educates us about the unpredictable and sometimes unfair results even after putting in extra efforts.

There always will be intelligent scholars who are broke, brilliant people without jobs, talented athletes who never accomplish desired glory and good authors whose books remain obscure. The reasons behind such an unfair marking/ grading system can be many, but some of the glaring ones can be ascertained to be attitude problems, communication issues, bad financial management and lack of soft skills besides plain old bad luck sometimes. Life has a strange way of teaching things for sure.

Positive aspect of life with respect to the grading system is that in the school we need to get "A" almost every time to be successful whereas in life it only takes one great "A" to be successful. We need to find this subject of our interest, achieving one great "A" in subject will make our life successful.

Today is the result of our past. Are we taking right steps to be successful tomorrow?

Who we are:

We were essentially a sort of chimpanzee like creature around six million years ago. First evolutionary step was the origin of bipedalism. Our very first ancestors appear to have been biped Apes that basically walked on two legs.

Another major shift occurred around four million years ago with Lucy, a very famous australopith. She had adapted to more open habitats and eating diets other than just fruits all day long.

Three million years ago we had started hunting and gathering naturally available food. Our brains got bigger, people started cooperating and processing their food. They also started running.

Homo erectus grew bigger brains and even larger bodies.

Final major shift was the origin of our own species i.e. Homo Sapiens. We're basically very much like our ancestors except we differ primarily above the neck. This change had a major effect on the entire world. We started communicating using verbal language.

History of the mankind showcases our adaptability towards the need based skill sets. We had learned running, hunting, farming, thinking and communicating as basic skill sets over the period of thousands of years of continuous evolution. We have developed complex emotions, need for comfort and taste for food. We have started seeking more and more comfort for our bodies at minimum work and efforts.

We have learnt reading very recently in 3000 B.C. but it's only in the 19th century that the universal literacy started to explode. These are some of the skill sets that we had acquired over the period of thousands of years.

From skillset development and employability perspective, first mass change happened around 1784 when the Steam powered engines started mass mechanical industries. The skill sets required during this period were knowledge of operating steam powered engines and machines for mechanical production. The second shift in the skill set development took place in the late 19th century, when electricity based mass production started. Skillsets required for this phase were skilled manpower to take care of manufacturing on large scale. People got into organized way of functioning and forming separate groups and departments with special manufacturing related skill sets. In the fourth quarter of the 20th century, electronics and automated production took off along with Information technology.

Looking at these timelines, we can very easily conclude that while the speed of growth was slow, we could develop necessary skillsets over the period of time. Once the skill sets were developed, we could take advantages of these skill sets over a period of long time. One could easily survive his entire professional career based on a single skill set. There was no need to learn more than one or two skillsets during the entire professional life of an individual.

Fortunately or unfortunately, we are currently moving at a very fast pace towards a technological revolution which is set to unsettle everything we have learned and practiced till now. The skill sets required for this dramatic change in the technology are still not very clear but they will eventually be radically different from the present skill sets. It means, the workforce of the tomorrow will have to learn and relearn different skill sets at a very fast speed. Surviving an entire professional career based on academic qualification and one or two acquired skills will not be possible. We'll have to be vigilant, agile and proactive in understanding the demands of the new workplace.

Compared to previous mass skill sets upheavals, this time we will have to be ready with the basic life skills so that advanced niche skill sets can be immediately acquired to take advantage of the upcoming growth opportunity.

Going by the discussions taking place in the industry circles, we are looking at a Fourth Industrial Revolution. The scorching pace at which technical breakthroughs are taking place around the globe is unprecedented in the history of mankind.

As per the Industry experts and World Economic Forum, we are on the brink of the Fourth Industrial Revolution. This revolution will encompass entire systems of production, management and governance across the industries on a global scale.

The inroads made by telecom and IT software/hardware has completely changed the landscape of human and Business related interactions and processes. Especially in the last decade, we can see extremely deep penetration of mobile connectivity and Internet services. Billions of people are connected on the common platform, communicating with each other. Executing business on these platforms seamlessly, we have got connected to people across the globe at a click of a mouse or at a click of a mobile phone. This enormous power of reach and collaboration with people in large numbers across the globe was never available with our ancestors.

Industrial leaders are very closely monitoring these emerging technology breakthroughs with abated breath. The areas of immediate interest and intense scrutiny are Internet Of Things (IoT), Genomics, Artificial Intelligence, Robotics, 3-D Printing, Autonomous Vehicles, Nano Technology, BioTechnology, Big Data and Analytics.

We can already see Tesla Motors and their counterparts evaluating their driverless cars (autonomous vehicles) on some specific American highways or elsewhere. The obvious question that comes to my mind is that what will happen to semi educated or uneducated drivers who are earning their livelihood by driving various vehicles. Of course the change will not happen overnight but how are we going to make sure that the transition of the Human to Autonomous is smooth and the affected people get sufficient time to alter their profession by acquiring new skill in the changed world? Who will help them learn the new skills?

Disruptive changes happening at a very fast rate

Vast amount of resources spent on Research and Development of cutting age technologies are changing the landscape of the Manufacturing, Transport, Computing and Connectivity. Advances made in the fields of Artificial Intelligence, 3D Printing, Internet of Things, Big Data and Analytics, Genomics, to name just a few, are changing the traditional work methods and performance parameters. SMART systems have become a buzzword, SMART HOMES, SMART CITIES, SMART MANUFACTURING PLANTS will make us rethink our methods of functioning and problem solving.

These technology implementations will have a huge impact on the way most employers are hiring their employees, most work profiles will change drastically. To start with, general administration and mundane routine work will be automated and other work profiles will undergo a sea change with respect to skill sets required to complete the predefined tasks.

Disruptive changes to various business models will make some jobs redundant while creating new job profiles along the way. The focus will shift to lesser human intervention, automation and improvement in employee productivity. We can think of similar shift which took place in India in the late nineteen nineties. Jobs related to manufacturing were the most coveted jobs in the industry. All the talented and scholar students were joining the manufacturing industry leaders or their ancillary units. Electronics and Mechanical fields were the most sought after streams of engineering. In the late nineties, things started to change when global Information Technology companies started recruiting talented candidates for their INDIA operations. IT companies were ready to pay significantly more salary than traditional manufacturing big-wigs. Students with strong academic qualifications used this opportunity and got better paying jobs with huge scope of career growth and wider global exposure.

These kind of software programming or system design or hardware related jobs were unheard of till late nineties. But huge section of the aspiring young population got an opportunity of riding the IT wave and catapult their careers on the information super highway.

We can observe similar patterns of mismatch wherein students while in school or colleges were not aware of the kind of jobs that will be made available to them by the changes taking place elsewhere in the globe.

In such a fluid employment scenario, the ability to anticipate and prepare ourselves for future skill set requirements is going to be extremely critical for individuals, industries and even governments. For government, it becomes even more critical to anticipate these changes and plan for the changing employment dynamics especially when large section i.e. 28% of Indian population is in the bracket of 10-24 year age group.

All the past changes in the demographics and technological breakthroughs have resulted into increased productivity, job creation and resultant personal and social growth. We can repeat these success stories provided we can foresee upcoming changes and take corrective proactive actions to get ready for the change.

What are these new demons? I mean domains?

Let us have a look at some of the areas of advanced technology innovations happening around the globe. These technologies are going to change the way we do our business and the way we lead our daily lives.

Big data analytics

Big Data is a phrase used to mean a massive volume of both structured and unstructured data that is so large that it is difficult to process using traditional database and software techniques. In most enterprise scenarios, the volume of data is too big or it moves too fast or it exceeds current processing capacity.

Big Data has the potential to help companies improve operations and make faster, more intelligent decisions. This data, when captured, formatted, manipulated, stored, and analyzed can help a company gain useful insight to increase revenues, get or retain customers, and improve operations.

To analyze such a large volume of data, big data analytics is typically performed using specialized software tools and applications for predictive analytics, data mining, text mining, forecasting and data optimization. Using big data tools and software enables an organization to process extremely large volumes of data that a business has collected to determine which data is relevant and can be analyzed to drive better business decisions in the future.

Artificial intelligence

Artificial intelligence is the branch of computer science concerned with making computers behave like humans.

Artificial intelligence includes the following areas of specialization:

Games Playing: programming computers to play games against human opponents

Expert Systems: programming computers to make decisions in real-life situations (for example, some expert systems help lawyers sift through huge piles of data to find relevant information on the particular legal issue or case)

Natural Language: programming computers to understand natural human languages

Neural Networks: Systems that simulate intelligence by attempting to reproduce the types of physical connections that occur in animal brains. (For example, some neural network systems are helping patients control and use the robotic arms and legs by their brains)

Robotics: Programming computers to see, hear and react to other sensory stimuli

IoT (Internet of Things)

IoT is short for Internet of Things. The Internet of Things (IoT) refers to the ever-growing network of physical objects that feature an IP address for internet connectivity, and the communication that occurs between these objects and other Internet-enabled devices and systems.

IoT Extends Internet Connectivity. The Internet of Things extends internet connectivity beyond traditional devices like desktop and laptop computers, smartphones and tablets to a diverse range of devices and everyday things that utilize embedded technology to communicate and interact with the external environment, all via the Internet.

Genomics

Genomics is a study of the genomes of organisms. Its main task is to determine the entire sequence of DNA or the composition of the atoms that make up the DNA and the chemical bonds between the DNA atoms. Knowledge of the DNA sequence has become an important part of biological research but it is also of vital importance in other research areas including medicine, biotechnology, forensic, etc.

3D printing

3D Printing is an additive manufacturing process that creates a physical object from a digital design. There are different 3D printing technologies and materials you can print with, but all are based on the same principle: a digital model is turned into a solid three-dimensional physical object by adding material layer by layer.

Nanotechnology

Nanoscience and nanotechnology are the study and application of extremely small things and can be used across all the other science fields, such as chemistry, biology, physics, materials science, and engineering. Today's scientists and engineers are finding a wide variety of ways to deliberately make materials at the nanoscale to take advantage of their enhanced properties such as higher strength, lighter weight, increased control of light spectrum, and greater chemical reactivity than their larger-scale counterparts.

Biotechnology

Biotechnology is the use of biological processes, organisms, or systems to manufacture products intended to improve the quality of human life. The earliest biotechnologists were farmers who developed improved species of plants and animals by cross pollination or cross breeding.

Quantum computing

Quantum computing is the area of study focused on developing computer technology based on the principles of quantum theory, which explains the nature and behavior of energy and matter on the quantum (atomic and subatomic) level. The quantum computer, following the laws of quantum physics, would gain enormous processing power through the ability to be in multiple states, and to perform tasks using all possible permutations simultaneously.

All the above mentioned technologies are very new from the point of industrial application perspective. Industrial leaders and scientists are working around the clock on practical applications of these technologies. The industrial grade application of these technologies will completely transform the Manufacturing and consumption patterns.

Human aspect of this disruptive change will also be guided by percentage of young population, rising middle class, early adoption of technology and improved purchasing power of this segment.

As per industry reports and World Economic Forum estimates, some of the existing employment generators will fall behind and new generators will take over resulting into larger skills gap. Some of the growth areas which will continue with their momentum are Architecture and Engineering, Computer and mathematical jobs. Some of the areas will decline such as manufacturing and Production roles and a significant decline on Office and Administrative roles. The manufacturing and production roles are expected to downsize due to technologies such as AI, IoT, Robotics and 3D printing improving the productivity and business profits manifold.

The strongest employment growth in the sector is expected from exploding online shopping and the application of Big Data analytics. Large manufacturing, FMCG and retail companies will use Big Data Analytics to collect, analyze and act upon insights from customer data and preferences to provide a personalized shopping experience.

The biggest drop in the employment is expected in Office and Administrative roles, which are expected to be negatively affected by technological trends that have the potential to make many of these job profiles redundant, such as mobile internet and cloud technology, Big Data analytics and the Internet of Things.

Improving employability?

Let us take a look at the way in which people can be skilled, nurtured and utilized across the employment sectors.

A lot of different groups of people and Industries are developing and executing their strategies focused on the year 2020.

Forces of technical advances and rapid globalization are fundamentally transforming the way in which business used to take place. The raw pace of this rapid change is generating a completely new set of job opportunities while making some of the skill sets completely or partially redundant. Going by the technologies in focus and the relevant skill sets required for the same, we can very safely assume that 1 out of 3 skillsets deployed today will need to be updated with a completely different skill set in the coming 4-5 years.

The systems of education and training have been developed many years ago. These systems are not being able to meet the challenge of supplying or training people for the new needs of the industry. The situation is changing so fast that it is estimated that by the time a 5 year old child completes his formal education, the types of jobs that will be available for him or her will be completely different from the type of jobs we see around us presently. These new work profiles will demand a very different type of skill sets which are not taught in most of the schools. On the other hand, adults who are working on the current profiles, will have to acquire these new skillsets in a very short span of time. To understand this point, let us consider Autonomous Vehicles i.e. driverless cars are expected to be used extensively in the coming 3- 4 years. The drivers who are currently driving these cars will be jobless and they will have to look for other means of earning their livelihood. If a person is earning his livelihood by driving as a profession for 10-12 years and is suddenly asked to stop driving and look for other job, this can be a difficult situation for him. He will have to either compromise while getting a driving related but less significant job or he will have to acquire a new skill set which will help him earn his livelihood.

The immediate step that can help us address the skillset gap is improving Primary education system with very frequently updated subject matter. Basic digital literacy is a need of the hour. We need to make sure that the potential candidates for the employment in the market should have basic understanding of the digital skills and its proper utilization to improve communication and efficiency.

We have been following the method of learning a skillset once and building our entire career on the same skillset without having to acquire new skillset. We can observe these things all around us. Let us say an individual graduates from the college and gets a job based on his college degree. Once he gets his job, he keeps on doing the same stuff till he gets retired. In the current scenario, we may not have the luxury of surviving our entire careers on a single skillset. We will have to keep on updating our knowledge and skillsets from time to time as per the market demands. We do not have organized systems of adult training or retraining like schools are available for children.

Our beliefs about schools and education are based on Education for Employment and Job Security. Both these terms have helped us reach the point where we are standing today. Unfortunately the shift in the workforce skillsets in a very short period of time are pushing us towards a point wherein we will have to recalibrate our beliefs. We'll have to look at education as a lifelong process of acquiring skillsets for Career Security instead of job security. Education for employment is not sufficient, education for Employability will serve our purpose in this turbulent marketplace.

It is estimated that one in every three skillsets acquired by an employee will be redundant. Technologies such as robotics, AI, IoT, will take care of these functions more efficiently at a much lower cost. It means, the people who will lose their jobs will have to find a new job based on new skillset.

When, where & how do we start?

Considering the situation we are in, we need to ask ourselves following questions. We need to ask ourselves, if I am confident that the skillsets which I am currently practicing at my workplace will take me through my entire career? If the answer is yes, we have not understood the issue at hand. If the answer is no, we need to immediately start identifying a new skill set which we must acquire within a specific timeframe.

Second question we need to ask ourselves is this, do I really believe that our children will be able to get a job or do something on their own using their current system of education? If the answer is yes, we are naïve about the situation around us and if the answer is no, we need to find out about what needs to be done to arm our children with relevant skillsets. The next obvious question is to find out where can we get the help in doing so?

CHAPTER 2

SOFT SKILLS ARE HARD TO FIND

What is the reason behind acute shortage of Soft skills in the workplace or in the public/private life? Soft skills are deteriorating across generations. Why this cultural phenomenon? How is it affecting us? and most importantly what are we going to do about it?

Soft skills are very closely associated with Emotional Intelligence (EI), which is the awareness and management of our own emotions, and the awareness and empathy for the emotions of others. EI drives soft skills because as messages enter our brain they first pass through the Limbic System which is where we experience stimuli emotionally. This system has helped us throughout our ancient civilization when we were surrounded by dangers. Our surroundings are comparatively very safe now. Our systems are tuned in such a way that if we would hear a growl which summoned the emotional reaction of fear, our Limbic System quickly sends a message to our legs along with a shot of adrenaline, to RUN! This is our default setting.

With the progress we have made as human beings, we are facing a peculiar issue now which is, now that our environment is relatively safe, we are training our limbic systems to react based on thoughtful response instead of emotional knee jerk response. Emotional intelligence is our ability to decide which messages should be given preference depending on their severity or critical nature, knowing which messages require a careful response vs. an emotional reaction. The more information we take in, the faster the need to process it, and the more we depend on emotional reactions and cognitive biases to get through our days.

Technical revolution is putting enormous pressure on this system of emotional reactions and cognitive biases. We are putting huge pressure on our brain's data processing capacity by feeding massive amount of data daily. This huge increase in information processing is making us react emotionally when often we should actually respond conscientiously. The result of this constant emotional reaction is poorer and poorer social or "soft" skills. It is also making an impact on our ability to focus given the constant distractions caused by social network and 24x7 electronic media. Information Overflow is overheating our brain processors resulting into degradation in the performance levels.

Technology is changing our world for the better. The benefits and convenience that have changed our world for the better are astounding and unprecedented, however, we need to pause and find a way to put our gadgets down temporarily to allow our brains to function the way they are intended to function.

Emotional intelligence is more important now than ever. Emotional intelligence skills can be improved through active participation in focused trainings, giving time to think about our behavior with others, and improving mindfulness techniques among other techniques. It will help all of us harvest our brain power in its most natural way to acquire skills which are necessary to succeed in the personal or professional lives.

Biggest challenge to economic progress

As an example, while managing our financial transactions with banks, beyond the technical skills, we always prefer working with banks who have pleasant and helpful staff. We tend to be even loyal to certain institutes wherein we are treated properly. On the other hand, our clients end up helping us even after making some mistakes in product or service delivery from our side, if we treat them properly and keep them proactively informed about certain issues. People overlook minor lacunae in the service, provided they don't get a feeling that they are being exploited or cheated.

We have highly skilled people who have been praised all over the world for their work ethic. One group of skills that is needed to boost our economy and be ready for the upcoming global challenges is soft skills.

Across all sectors of our economy the technical skills required to handle any job are available. Most of individual contributors or team members or team leaders however lack the skills to manage people. This problem is aggravated by the fact that people management skills are not taught as a life skill. Universities and colleges teach human resources management which is not the same as people management.

Most professionals lack the emotional intelligence to handle people at an emotional level. Lack of such skills has led to discomfort and discontent in many organizations.

Why soft skills matter?

While our technical skills may get our foot in the door, our people skills will open most of the doors to come. Our work ethic, our attitude, our communication skills, our emotional intelligence and a whole host of other personal attributes are the soft skills that are crucial for successful career.

With these soft skills we can excel as a leader. Problem solving, delegating, motivating, and team building are all much easier if you have good soft skills. Knowing how to get along with people – and displaying a positive attitude – are crucial for success.

The importance of these soft skills is grossly undervalued, and there is far less training provided for these skills compare to hard skills. For some reason, organizations seem to expect people know how to behave on the job. They tend to assume that everyone knows and understands the importance of being on time, taking initiative, being friendly, and producing high quality work.

Assuming that soft skills are universal leads to much frustration. That's why it's so important to focus as much on soft skills training and development as we do on traditional hard skills.

The soft skills gap – do you have one?

When our workforce has excellent technical skills but limited soft skills, organizations cannot utilize their potential to the fullest. If the organization is successful in acquiring new clients but is not able to retain them, chances are that we have a soft skills gap. If our organization has lots of staff turnover and we end up keeping them training again and again, chances are that we have a soft skill gap.

In fact, whenever we are unable to capitalize on the wealth of knowledge, experience and proficiency within our team, then we should be assessing the level of communication and interpersonal skills that are present in our organization.

The workplace has an evolved interpersonal dynamic that can't be ignored. The acts of listening, presenting ideas, resolving conflict, and inspiring an open and honest work environment all comes down to knowing how to build and maintain relationships with people. It's those relationships that allow people to participate fully in team projects, show appreciation for others, and enlist support for their projects.

It's important for us to recognize the vital role soft skills play within our team and not only work on developing them within yourself, but encourage their development throughout the organization. Areas to examine and evaluate include: Personal accountability, ability to collaborate, Interpersonal negotiation skills, Conflict resolution, adaptability and flexibility, the clarity of communications, Creative thinking, Inclusive attitude, Coaching and mentoring skills.

The more of these things we see around us, the better people's soft skills are likely to be within our organization. These all have a significant impact on the attitude a person brings to interactions with clients, customers, colleagues, supervisors, and other stakeholders. The more positive someone's attitude is, the better that person's relationships will be. That's what motivates great team performance, and leads people to contribute strongly to the organization's growth and prosperity.

Soft skills are increasingly becoming the most visible differentiating factor between a successful person and a person who is not able to live up to his full potential. It's just not enough to be highly trained in technical skills, without developing the softer, interpersonal and relationship-building skills that help people to communicate and collaborate effectively.

These people skills are more critical than ever as society and industries struggle to find meaningful ways to remain competitive and be productive. Teamwork, leadership, and communication are underpinned by soft skills development. Since each is an essential element for organizational and personal success, developing these skills is very important and is almost indispensable now!

Schools and training institutes are trying to work together with the industries to provide relevant soft skills trainings but the gap between the demand and availability of these skillsets if widening day by day. Institutes are revising their curriculum based on market demands though the speed at which they can incorporate these changes is not sufficient.

In some cases, the work profile is getting complex due to usage of technology and automation. On the other hand, due to availability of well-educated candidates and limited number of job opportunities, companies and organization can hire these well-educated personnel for entry level jobs. We can often come across situations wherein post graduates are now applying for junior clerk or peon level jobs.

The skill set deficiency has started affecting the industries, government organizations and social sectors in terms of employee productivity, customer satisfaction and profitability. On the other hand, employees are also feeling the heat due to ever widening gap in the skill sets they possess and the ones their work profile demands. It results into lesser job satisfaction, drop in productivity levels and increase in job related stress.

Cumulative effect of these gaps is failure of individuals and companies to utilize their resources to the optimum level. In turn, it is adversely affecting the growth of the economy. Industrial powerhouses and organizations have started working on their own to create various skill based trainings available to colleges and institutes. They are conducting routine seminars and workshops in schools and universities to keep these young people informed about the changes happening in the industry along with generation of relevant skillsets demand. It is helping these students or aspiring candidates understand the areas in which they can build and hone their skillsets upon for better employment opportunities.

It is estimated that in the next five years, over one-third of skills that are considered important today will undergo a sea change. These sweeping changes will completely alter the way we conduct business, and the way we go about our lives. Existing job profile and skills required to perform those jobs will be changed drastically. New job profiles with completely different set of skillsets requirements will get generated.

Out of syllabus, out of sight & out of mind

Let us have a look at the most important skill sets which will form the backbone of the modern Work-force along with Technical competence in advanced technologies:

Modern workspace is changing very rapidly. Typical tools of work in these environments are digital files of different types, different applications catering to information gathering, processing, management, applications catering to enhance efficiency of the employees, applications used for corporate or professional communication, applications used for tracking, monitoring and supervising progress of different work related activities etc.

Mere technical knowledge of specific area of work like accountancy or sales or purchase or technical skills of designing and producing high quality products is not going to suffice the work profile demands. A lot of different skillsets and efforts will be an essential part delivering modern day key role assignments of the workforce.

Let us understand what these skills are and how are they going to help us navigate rapidly changing workplaces:

Document management

In a modern workspace, majority of the business communication and collaboration will be revolving around sharing information with each other in the form of digital files and documents.

Most of the job profiles need an understanding of the entire ecosystem of digital files, applications/softwares used for creating, storing, managing, securing, analyzing, reporting these digital files and multiple user interfaces used to access relevant data in these digital files.

Very limited work profiles will be based on manual labor and with nothing to do with digital data. Obviously we are working towards improving literacy rates across the globe, but large number of people still are illiterate.

Amazingly enough, after huge penetration of telecommunication devices in India in the last 10 odd years coupled with remarkably easy to use interfaces in these smart devices, almost everybody even illiterate people can use and operate these devices very easily. Whole new world of information and possibilities has opened up for them.

Especially voice services made possible by these telecom devices like mobile phones or information kiosks in rural areas, has reduced a great deal of effort and time of these disadvantaged people who could not write or read. A completely new way of finding information which was hitherto available only for the people who could read or write is transforming the way people are working.

Hence understanding complete lifecycle of data will prove an extremely important advantage to the people. It will help reduce the time to decision, time lost in execution due to poor communication and errors in analysis of the data.

Project delivery and execution

The ability of an individual to work in a team towards delivering a project of any kind and size by working together, collaborating with each other is an important skill set. The project can be a business project or a social project. In a modern workplace, an individual will have to understand and learn to use the processes and systems put in place by organizations to improve coordination and teamwork towards successful and timely execution of the deliverables.

Delegation of work, follow-up of the activities, and interdepartmental coordination backed up by strong technical knowledge will largely make or break new digital workplace success stories.

Employees of tomorrow will have to don both the hats of an individual performer and a strong team player.

Prioritization, attention to detail

Proliferation of Internet and smart devices have exposed us to technology 24 hours of the day. We are bombarded continuously with more and more data. Social networking is dumping mostly irrelevant data on us.

This continuous barrage of data is distracting us from our core set of duties and responsibilities. Our capacity to process the data and make well informed decisions has not necessarily increased in the proportion of this deluge of data. Hence our capacity to complete our tasks by focusing on particular set of activities without getting distracted is getting hampered seriously.

The skill of deciding which stream of data is important for us and focusing on these streams to complete the tasks and blocking other disturbances is a very important tool of enhancing our productivity. Managing our time and attention by prioritizing tasks/objectives and completing them efficiently within stipulated timeframe is a most in demand skill set today. This skill set can be supported or improved by methods like Mindfulness.

Lack of this skillset will certainly prove to be a biggest weakness of an individual not only from employability perspective but also from personal growth and success angle.

Communication

Communication skills is a very important and well discussed topic till date. Verbal and Non-verbal communication plays an extremely important role in achieving personal and professional goals. Along with traditional ways of communication, digital communication is becoming a very important tool in the modern workplace.

Most of the communication taking place between an employee and his employer or customer is taking place in the form of emails or telephonic calls or video-conferences.

Lack of this skillset will certainly prove to be a biggest weakness of an individual not only from employability perspective but also from personal growth and success angle. Hence effective and timely communication with the clients or other stakeholders will shape the relationship between the client and the business.

Netiquettes / telequettes / digital etiquettes

Etiquettes are basically socially acceptable norms of behavior.

In a global workplace of today and tomorrow most of the interactions that will take place will be in the form of Emails or Telephonic calls or video-conferences. Due to time and distance constraints, it will not be practical and economical to meet all the people face to face all the time. Hence most of the people who will be interacting with us will judge us or form an opinion about us by observing our emails and telephonic calls.

Our personality and characters are judged by social and personal etiquettes by default. An important addition of one more form of etiquette which can build or destroy our image/reputation or brand is Netiquettes or Telequettes or Digital Etiquettes.

Let us understand what these digital etiquettes are:

Internet and modes of fast transportation have bought us together at a very fast pace. We no longer have to wait for sending or receiving messages from our loved ones or colleagues. Internet or Intranet is our new Society. Netiquette refers to the socially acceptable rules of communication and behavior when we are communicating with each other on the internet. New hubs of social interactions are emails, blogs, online portals, social networking sites etc.

Let us start with the basic steps:

Very important aspect of writing emails, is their timing. We should avoid writing emails when we are under tremendous pressure or stress. Under such a circumstances, we tend to respond emotionally rather than practically and the message can get misinterpreted due to lack of complete attention while writing the emails.

Emails should be responded promptly.

Mails should be self-explanatory.

Subject line should reflect the message of the email. Long and complicated subject line tends to confuse the recipient. People tend to ignore emails with unclear subject lines.

Emails should start with formal greetings.

Be crisp. Lengthy emails need a lot of time to read. Lengthy emails are ignored and the actual message gets lost. Intention of writing the email gets defeated.

Basic grammatical mistakes such as punctuation marks, capital letters should be avoided. Capital letters should be used sparingly only to highlight most critical words and points.

Never deviate from the topic. Addressing multiple topics in a single email should be avoided.

Typical guidelines of creating paragraphs, avoiding long sentences, using bullet-point should be followed.

All the relevant stakeholders should be marked in the emails.

All official emails should have signatures at the bottom. We tend to assume that the recipient knows our contact details. But making them handy doesn't hurt. Signature should include name, contact numbers, email ID and designation. Signatures with wrong information should be strictly avoided.

Emails are documented proofs. We should avoid writing offensive or abusive emails.

Some companies have fixed font styles for email communications. It helps maintain uniformity in the organizational communication. Fancy fonts, sizes and colors should be avoided.

Keep the emails restricted to concerned personnel only. Adding irrelevant people in the email is not recommended due to information security reasons besides wastage of time.

All the emails marked to you should be replied. Person sending you an email expects at least acknowledgement of receipt of the message. Very frequently, people don't read all the emails due to whatever reasons and brag about their busy schedules. It is basically a complete lack of seriousness and time management. By not reading emails, we are implying that your emails are of no value to me.

The language and the tone of the email should be polite and formal. Short forms and abbreviations should be avoided when recipients are from different departments or backgrounds.

Avoid personal comments in official email communications.

Avoid attaching heavy files in emails. Downloading them consumes a lot of bandwidth. Use other media like CD or USB drives or wireless local area networks for such large size file transfers.

Information Security aspects of email communications are very critical. Email exchanges are the main source of online security threats such as malwares, spam mails, phishing attempts and virus infections.

Telephone etiquettes:

After understanding about Netiquettes, let us now go through Telephone Etiquettes

The telephone is a communication device which uses widely deployed telecommunication infrastructure to make incoming/outgoing voice calls, sending receiving SMS and providing data connectivity solutions with technologies like 5G, 4G VoLTE, 3G etc. Telephone etiquette is basically related to voice calls made over short and long distance. This method of communications is so deeply entrenched in our business and personal communication now that the old methods of sending post cards and letters using Post Offices looks like an ancient history.

Telephonic conversations makes keeping in touch and doing business both efficient and easy. Whether at the office, in transit, or at home, we use it to keep in touch with colleagues, make meeting arrangements, or broker business deals.

Displaying proper telephone etiquette is an essential part of setting yourself ahead of other job seekers.

Telephonic conversation skills are important for everybody irrespective of his age or education of profession or background.

Let us have a look at some of the basic etiquettes while using telephone:

Answering the phone after two or three rings with a friendly business like greeting is a better way of starting a conversation.

Posture of body is very important while talking on the phone. If you can standup straight and have gentle Smile on your face while talking on the phone, Callers can hear your pleasantness, cheerfulness, and eagerness to do sincere business with him, even if they can't see you.

If answering the phone for a colleague. Get the name of the caller before transferring the call or handing it over to the recipient. If the recipient is busy and is expected to take more than 30 seconds, inform the caller about the same and ask him if he can hold or he is ok with recipient calling him back once he is free.

If you answer the phone for someone else, there is no need to explain why he or she can't answer the phone. Simply say that your colleague is away from his or her desk or the office.

Don't talk with food or gum in your mouth.

Speak clearly and slowly.

Most phones have voice mail. Make sure your message for incoming calls sounds professional. Example: Hello, you've reached Neelesh Kajale. I'm not available to take your call. Please leave your name and number after tone and I'll return your calls as soon as possible. Please make sure to return the calls, once you are available.

If you will be out of the office for an extended period. Change your voice mail message to give callers instructions on alternate ways to reach you or your colleague or your boss who can take care of your business in your absence.

When making calls, introduce yourself right away so the recipient knows whom they are talking with. Example: "Hello, this is Neelesh Kajale calling. Is Mr. Andrew Bale available?"

When leaving a message, speak slowly. Repeat your name so that the recipient has time to write it down without replaying the message.

Speak directly into the mouthpiece. Using a headset is a better option if you have to use computer or any other device while having a conversation.

If someone walks into your office while you're talking on the phone, ask the caller if you may put him/her on hold briefly.

Don't place the handset or mobile phone on the desk without disconnecting the call or without putting the call on hold. There is a chance of the person on the call listening your conversation while he is on the call.

Screening the calls is important sometimes. If we are required to ask who is calling or what the nature of the call is, we need to be aware of our tone of voice. Screening calls results into offending the caller sometimes, if not handled properly.

Taking phone messages should cover name of the person for whom the message is left. Caller's name, company department and number. Date and time of the call, Message to be given, action to be taken such as "Pls call" or "Urgent". Point also to be noted is understanding his availability to attend the call. Critical part is to deliver the message as soon as possible with all the relevant details while maintaining confidentiality.

If we have to leave a message on a voice mail, leave the message with the information such as your name, department and contact number, date and time with the message including a good time to reach you.

For closing the conversation, thank the caller for taking a time and calling. Summarize the actionable and follow up timeframes and deadlines. Thank them for calling and say "Good-Bye".

Basic underlying telephone etiquette is Courtesy. If the caller is a potential customer and we are courteous to him, we have an excellent chance of gaining a new client. If he is an existing client, we'll keep him for life. On the other hand, if we fail to be courteous to people, there are very high chances of losing the person without any further deliberations.

Information gathering and screening

Digital information about every subject is available on the internet. Skills required for the modern workforce are to gather authentic information from trusted sources like internet or company internal databases.

Huge amount of archived digital data is available across internet sites and depositories. The skill is knowing about where to search for the relevant data and how to glean the information from the available raw information.

In the age of information overload, without the information gathering and screening skills, we cannot effectively and efficiently tap into mountain of digital data and make sure that the outcome is an authentic, relevant, and dependable information which can be used for decision making.

Modern business tools literacy

Modern businesses are based on different tools used for automating business processes, to increase productivity and quality of the products and services. Multiple applications, softwares, operating systems, hardware devices are part of this vast setup.

For a modern employee, to be successful in this complex web of different technologies and devices, he or she must have understanding of how all these things work together and their dependencies. Lack of understanding of these business systems will prove to be a serious handicap for people to start with.

Security, privacy and action accountability

Security threats to businesses are increasingly sophisticated and business losses due to these attacks are very heavy. Most common reason of security breach is Human error. Lack of awareness about how proprietary data and company intellectual property needs to be protected is causing the most severe damage to the businesses.

Lack of Security and Privacy awareness is making businesses bleed money worldwide. Businesses are taking various steps to monitor and report security breaches so that concerned personnel can be held accountable for their careless actions.

Awareness of security, privacy related standard guidelines will be an added skill which will certainly help us get better job and employment opportunities.

Assertiveness & independence

To be assertive is to understand that everyone has basic human rights that should be respected and upheld. We need a balance between responding passively and behaving aggressively. Responding passively may result in such rights to be neglected or ignored, whereas behaving aggressively tends to abuse the rights of other.

Diplomacy

Knowing what to say and what mot to say with a keen sense of timing can help us avoid conflict and hurtful feelings. Tact and Diplomacy helps us achieve our goals while maintaining good relations.

Global outlook

It is about developing necessary skillsets and behavioral patterns to match Global standards and performance requirements without losing our basic strengths and objectives. It helps us build confidence to work in global businesses and seize opportunities.

As cultural and business complexity increases so does the demand for a global mindset. Global outlook is the ability to influence individuals, groups, and organizations that have different intellectual, social belief systems and work ethics from our own. We must improve our understanding of local and cultural differences. It requires recognizing situations in which demands from both global and local elements are compelling, while being aware of the diversity across cultures and markets.

Economic development activity is shifting globally. The availability of skilled personnel and the shift of knowledge based industries are changing the business dynamics. Corporate and industrial geographical limitations are getting blurred. In these changing circumstance, we should be open to global ideas and ways of implementing them.

Situational awareness

Situational awareness refers to real-time information about what's happening in and around a given facility/campus/

enterprise. Considering the local and global security threats and situations, we must train ourselves to be aware of one's surroundings and identifying potential threats and dangerous situations.

It is more of a mindset than a hard skill. Because of this, situational awareness is not something that can be practiced only by highly trained government agents or specialized corporate security teams. Indeed, it can be exercised by anyone with the will and the discipline to do so. Situational awareness is not only important for recognizing terrorist threats, but it also serves to identify criminal behavior and other dangerous situations.

Collaboration

With the expansion of the information-service sector of the economy and the flattening of organizational hierarchies, interpersonal competencies such as oral communication, written communication, and the ability to collaborate, are becoming more and more important to employers.

Collaboration is a necessary skill which is the ability to relate well to others, the ability to cooperate and the ability to manage and resolve conflicts.

Collaboration is bringing the right people to the right projects at the right time. Competitive advantage is increasingly tied to collaborative advantage.

It is use of technology to impact workforces across the globe in the ways such as to make knowledge available when needed by whosoever regardless of their physical location, to provide for teleconferencing, videoconferencing, meetings, and application sharing by teams in far-flung corners of the world.

Critical thinking & problem solving

Critical thinking and Problem Solving is about making decisions under severe constraints. It is about evaluating multiple solutions and methods of handling specific situation along with ability to troubleshoot things when they go wrong.

Creativity & innovation

Innovation and creativity are new requirements of the modern workforce who are championing business in global markets. Many of us in the past may have been highly successful in some markets, but we are facing completely different challenges in today's emerging ones for which we are not prepared, may be.

Only by bringing our knowledge, skills, and experiences together, can today's workforce hope to successfully navigate the complexity of modern workplace. This requires us to be anything but traditional. We need to be flexible, creative, willing to change, and in fact, desire change and innovation.

Globalization requires creativity. Creativity requires deep knowledge of one area and broad knowledge of many others—plus the ability to see patterns and combine different elements in new ways. It thrives best among people who can think out of the box for path-breaking solutions.

Self sufficiency

Self-sufficiency is being able to take responsibility for one's own future and acting in self-directed, self- sufficient ways.

Cross cultural understanding

Organizations with a genuine global mindset, hold their employees accountable for inclusiveness. Such organizations ensure that their people are exposed to international issues and situations.

Understanding how to work with culturally diverse workplaces is one of the new assets global leaders must develop. Not only cultural diversity, but also employing more women in executive positions, attracting and motivating the most talented members of different backgrounds and cultures. We need to respect social beliefs and work ethics.

Social skills & intelligence

Understanding the socially acceptable behavioral patterns helps in developing more acceptable characteristics. It also helps us in avoiding getting into anti-social movements and activities. It helps us think rationally and avoid troublesome people and situations. We can use this skill to channelize our resources and energies for constructive work.

How to behave in a world wide web society?

Email is one of the gateways to the world of communication besides the web sites. The way we behave on the World Wide Web can have far reaching consequences. World Wide Web is a Wild Wild West without any nominated sheriff. Everybody is responsible for his or her safety and security. There are so many governing bodies controlling and monitoring the net but it is our collective responsibility to take care of our own safety and security.

Considering the alarming increase in the incidents related to cyber security in recent years and the sophistication with which these attacks are planned and implemented on global scale, it is extremely critical to know the boundaries of our safe neighborhood and basic rules of safe engagement with our most trusted internet neighbors, buddies, friends and foes.

Installing an Antivirus is not a solution to all the information security issues. Netiquettes are necessary for recognizing online threats and avoiding them at all costs.

More than 50% of internet attacks and security incidents are caused not by outsiders but our colleagues, former colleagues, current partners, former partners. That means more than half of the security attacks are perpetrated by the people whom we know very well.

Of all the security measures that can be planned and implemented, the most effective and basic tool is our personal, organizational and social awareness about security.

Let us go through some of the pointers which can help us manage our digital interactions in a better way:

Keep the interaction humane

It is extremely interesting to observe car drivers while driving on the road, curse at each other, make obscene gestures. The same car drivers will most probably never do it if they are face to face with each other. Inclusion of machine seems to change their behavior. Similarly, while we are interacting with other people on the internet, we tend to lose our handle very easily. We'll certainly be more polite and diplomatic if the other person is right in front us instead of behind the computer someplace unknown. The inclusion of machine makes us forget that the counterpart we are interacting with is a human being and not a machine.

Everything we post online is recorded and saved someplace safe. We do not have any control on where it will resurface and in what context. Any email or a message that we send, we have no control on where it goes.

We'll have to follow basic rules of courtesy and etiquettes of human interaction while interacting with the person on the other side of the IP address.

Extend your good personal character to your online interactions

In real life, most of us are people with good manners and good intentions. We need to behave in the same fashion while interacting with people online too. There are laws for cybersecurity and they are getting stronger day by day. Chances of getting away with a cybercrime are very less.

Just like cultures differ from state to state or from country to country, cyberspace also has its own cultures. Before participating in online discussions, it is better to watch for some time, observe what is acceptable and what is not and then we can jump into those interactions or conversations.

Time and bandwidth are costly

Time is the new money. It is the most sought after asset of this generation. Everybody seems to have no time because of their busy schedules and workloads. When we are participating in the online discussion, we should be careful of not wasting other's time by repeating the same things again and again. Time is wasted obviously but bandwidth required to carry the same message repeatedly is also a wastage.

Create an online mirror image

Online groups or discussion forums typically don't judge people by basic human criteria like skin tone, eyes, hair or weight, height or your clothing, shoes. They judge you by the content you share on these forums. If you are conversant with a certain subject, it will obviously reflect in your thoughts shared in the online community. It is better to be polite and pleasant rather than offensive and rude. Offensive behavior makes you shine for a moment in infamy and then you are ignored and left to fend for yourself. People just avoid you.

Improve your knowledge by sharing

Best part of online discussion forums and communities is their reach and sheer numbers. It is a collective intelligence present at a click of a button. If we are posting any query in a group, so many intelligent people are reading our question. Some of them who are conversant with the topic will answer our query. The collective information that we can get can be substantial.

Respect others privacy. Don't abuse your powers

System administrators having access to all the accounts should never read others private emails.

Keep all of our operating systems, softwares & applications updated. Remove all the applications, softwares which are not in use

Each and every OS, software or app needs regular updates and security fixes. Hackers and cybercriminals exploit bugs in these softwares before they are patched. Biggest issue is that most users never or rarely update their softwares.

Most of the softwares keep on communicating with their servers for their updates whether they are in use or not. These backdoors gets exploited time and again to break into softwares or operating systems.

Never open emails from unknown or dubious sources & if you have to, be extremely careful while opening them

Being suspicious of strangers goes a long way on the internet too. We should never trust emails from people we have never met. We should be even more careful when they ask us to click a link or open an innocent looking attachment.

While surfing the net, check the website addresses very seriously. An exact copy an official website with a very minor difference in the website address can be used to lure you into sharing your Internet banking username and password.

Simple message is to not reply to the emails from unknown sources, don't click on suspicious attachments and don't click on the links in the emails. Don't click on suspicious ads.

If it's free on the internet, be extra cautious

Just like in practical life, nothing should be assumed to be free without the strings attached to it. Typical free softwares are used to lure unsuspecting users into downloading malwares or viruses or dangerous applications which can share your confidential data with the hackers in the background without us ever coming to know about it until our systems break down.

We can use google to search about the free software and its reviews to ascertain the authenticity and safety of using the software.

Never share sensitive information online

Check your social networking profile settings. You will be surprised about the amount of your personal information that is shared with your consent. You have already given consent to use it without even knowing about it. You have accepted all the terms and conditions of these sites without reading them while registering yourself in the first place.

Improve social networking profile privacy and security immediately. Most of the time, they are by default "permit all deny none" settings. We need to change them to "Deny all, permit none" and then fine-tune them.

It is surprisingly easy to follow network profiles and collect a lot of personal information. We must be skeptical about people we meet online and about their intentions.

Keep your personal account information private

Due to increasing use of internet for various personal and professional activities, we keep on creating multiple accounts and profiles on various sites. Managing these profiles and remembering multiple username and passwords is extremely difficult. Using the same password for more than one site and profile is a sure recipe for disaster. If a hacker gets hold of your one account, your online presence can be compromised easily.

Reporting illegal & offending content

Using "Flag as spam" or "Flag as offensive" buttons for reporting offending and illegal activities.

Your online posts are forever

We keep on posting photos, comments, location updates and our favorite hobbies with personal details knowingly or unknowingly. Most of these posts even in private groups and forums are indexed for search. Search engines save and classify our activities on multiple online servers.

These companies are making necessary changes to decide timelines for online content after which it will be deleted permanently. But this is a slow reform and will take time and awareness among common users.

Always think twice before posting personal information or updates on the internet. Delete or edit all of your posts which reveal too much about you. Before posting anything anywhere on the WWW, check if this content can affect your personal or professional life in the future.

Use security tools & products before going online

Using good antivirus, antimalware, antispam solutions to prevent hackers from stealing your data is a better option. Things are changing very fast. Avoiding adult porn sites is not sufficient now. Hackers are hiding malicious code even in legitimate websites.

Back up all the important data

Be ready for the worst case scenario, always back up all our important files. It will help us survive any eventuality of a hard disk failure or a ransomware attack.

Digital mental disorder: cyberbullying

Advances in technology have helped us getting ourselves online in a matter of clicks in seconds. Anybody with internet access can participate in this large, global WWW (Wild Wild West). These developments are very positive, but they also have some negative and dangerous possibilities attached to this freedom of participation especially for innocent children accessing the internet.

In a typical neighborhood or society we grow in, there are good people, bad people and really nasty people all around us. People with bad intentions lurk around the corners waiting for a chance to attack us. Internet community also reflects the same patterns of human behavior. There are good people contributing immensely to collective knowledge and intelligence in the internet community. Then there are people with malicious intentions, who are waiting for us to expose our weaknesses online so that they can take advantage of our lack of awareness or plain stupidity.

Cyberbullying is a new age mental sickness in Internet community which is equivalent of social eIntimidation, abuse and misuse of privileges of being a cyber-citizen. It can be defined as a willful and deliberate online interaction carried out by an individual or a group of people using computers, mobile phones, or any other devices connected to internet.

Cyberbullying takes on many different forms. Exclusion, Harassment, Trolling, Flaming, Cyberstalking, Dissing, Fraping, Doxing, Griefing are some of the terms used to describe different types of cyberbullying. Cyberbullying can take place through emails, online discussion forums, social networking groups and sites, chatting groups and any other digital forms of communications where people can interact with each other.

Let us have a look at some of the types of digital abuse.

Exclusion is a deliberate attempt to exclude a certain individual from online groups.

Harassment is repeatedly sending malicious messages to someone online to disturb or intimidate him or her.

Trolling is a common form of cyberbullying in an online community such as social media or online gaming in order to elicit a reaction, disruption by starting arguments or upsetting people by posting inflammatory messages. Intention of trolling is to provoke readers into an emotional response.

Flaming is a typical online fight through emails or social networking groups or instant messaging apps where angry and rude messages with personal insults and comments are exchanged.

Cyberstalking is a continuous attempt made to establish contact with our without our consent. Cyberstalking is an extremely dangerous form of cyberbullying wherein adults use the internet to contact and attempt to meet with young people for sexual purposes which can have very serious consequences if not stopped immediately.

Dissing is the act of sharing or posting personal sensitive information about us online to damage our reputation or relationships with other. Most of the time dissing attempts are made by the people close to us, who know about us.

Fraping is when somebody logs into our social networking account and posts inappropriate messages or comments using our profiles.

Doxing or doxxing is collecting personal information of an individual such as home address, birthdate, contact information and private sensitive data and posting it online without his or her consent or knowledge.

Griefing is a new form of cyberbullying. It does not use email messages or social media. Griefing happens on interactive multiplayer online video games. It is a term used to describe a cyberbully causing frustration to the target individual and his/her friends by not following the rules of an interactive online video game.

There are so many things that can be used with malicious intents. We need to be careful and vigilant.

Cyberbullying a bigger threat

Cyberbullying risk is growing at a very fast rate. It can be a bigger threat than traditional bullying due to anonymity of users in the cyber space. Impersonation is very easy and fear of getting caught is minimal. These reasons are making more and more sick minds attempt cyberbullying.

Second biggest reason behind increase in cyberbullying incidents is lack of supervision. It is extremely difficult to supervise internet usage of an individual. We cannot monitor online activities of our children and others continuously.

Third important point is about the possibility of intimidating a victim at all the places whenever he comes online. Victims can run away from traditional bullying and go home where they are safe. Since most of us frequent users of internet at almost every place possible, victims are no longer safe even in their homes.

Fourth important aspect of cyberbullying is Humiliation. Social acceptance and online image are very important for us. Any use and circulation of sensitive or damaging videos or images can dent our image very fast. Sharing of these videos or images cannot be controlled in any way.

Timeless skill set: time management

What is time management?

It is a set of principles, practices, skills, tools and systems that help us use our time to accomplish our objectives.

Why is time management important?

Time is the most valuable asset for us. If we can consciously observe our working and time spending habits, we can understand how much of our time is actually utilized in efficient manner and how much of it gets wasted in useless activities? It creates a false notion of not having enough time to complete our tasks or for achieving our goals.

In the modern world, we can take help of technology and various methods of efficient time management. We need to first understand why managing time is important for us. Without understanding the importance of time management, we will not be able to achieve any positive results.

Let us understand why time management is crucial to our professional and personal well-being.

Limited availability of time - Everybody is allotted 24 hours per day. Nobody can have more time than this per day. We will have to find ways and means of utilizing this limited amount of time for producing better outcomes.

Accomplishing more with less efforts – Once we learn to take control of our time, we start focusing on improving our skillsets which in turn increases our efficiency.

Improved Decision Making – If we are pressed for time and are supposed to make important decisions in personal or professional matters, we tend to overlook some of the options available and make decisions without due diligence. Hurrying through decision making process affects quality of our decisions. By improving time management skills, we can avoid the pressure generated due to limited time and hence decisions taken can be more factual and correct.

Devoting Time To Learning New Skills – Time management is key to success. It helps us take control of our schedules and busy lives. Better time management can provide us with extra time which can be utilized for reading, learning and improving new things and skills. It can help us rest in a better way.

Stress Reduction And Free Time – All of us need time to relax and rest. Because of time management issues, we tend to keep on juggling various activities and tasks throughout our days. We keep on running between our jobs, families and other activities which saps all our energy. We end up feeling terrible and exhausted all the time. We can manage time better and save some time daily for our own self. We can spend some time with ourselves doing nothing. Even 10 minutes per day can be miraculous. It helps us reduce stress levels substantially. When we have the control of our time, we feel relaxed and can achieve better results.

Poor Health, Bad relationships - Most of us, feel like they have too much to do and not enough time. We always blame lack of time for our poor finances, stress, bad relationships, and for not exercising our body. Improved time management can help us find the time for what we desire, and for what we need to do.

Prioritizing – Time management helps us learn to find the time for things that are important to us. It helps us make deliberate decisions about prioritizing our tasks and activities.

Improving Productivity – Improved time management skills help us improve our efficiency by reducing wastage of energy and resources. It helps us become more creative and productive.

Avoiding Distractions – We have so many distraction in life. Internet, TV are consuming large portion of our daily lives. We need to ask ourselves, how spending time on these things is going to help us. If a certain activity is not adding any value to our life, it is better to stop wasting time on those activities. We can free up a lot of time and energy by taking proper actions on these distractions.

Detachment – A certain degree of detachment is useful in managing our time effectively. It helps us avoid spending our energy and time on things which doesn't matter to us like people's reactions to our actions or their perceptions about us. It can save a lot of our time since we tend to spend a lot of time and energy on thinking about what others will be thinking about us.

Reading, Planning – Thinking, planning and observing how successful people spend their time can be a better way of learning about time management. Reading books and articles on time management can also help us hone our skills.

Getting Up Early In The Morning –A lot of improvement can be observed just by waking up early in the morning. Even 15 minutes earlier can help us read, meditate, exercise or plan our day in advance. Giving up watching TV late at night and going to sleep a little earlier than usual will help us wake up on time without losing on the sleep cycle.

It is easy to see positive chain reaction of good time management skills. It helps us accomplish more in less time. Time saved can be used to learn new things, which in turn will help us identify and utilize new opportunities in a better way. Reduced stress levels helps us focus more on our tasks resulting into better outcomes in shortest period of time. Each benefit of time management improves some or the other aspect of our life.

Time management, when and where?

This brings us to basic question of when and where should we start focusing on to improve time management skills so that a lot of heartache of not achieving the goals even after working extremely hard can be avoided. A lot of energy can be saved and used for better purposes.

Adults with time management issues obviously need to immediately learn these skills but for creating better prospects for our youth and young generation, time management skills should be main focus even for the age brackets of 5-10 years and above. Planting the time management skills in the minds of kids will certainly help them in their lives and careers.

Time management skills will help children prioritize tasks and accurately judge amount of time needed to complete them. It inculcates the habit of estimating time required to finish certain task, it helps them monitor the progress of the task with a positive sense of urgency.

At home, these skills will help kids' complete daily chores and household work in a timely manner. It will help them with healthy habits of getting ready for school on time. It will help them eat their food at specific time daily. Children with poor time management skills will prove disastrous as they grow since they keep on making same mistakes again and again.

Time management skills will help kids answer their examination papers within stipulated time in a better way without leaving any questions unanswered. It will help them plan their assignments and play time schedules properly.

To conclude, sowing the seeds of proper skill sets in the minds of kids is the easiest way of avoiding a whole lot of wastage of human potential and energy.

CHAPTER 3

A SHORTCUT TO FAILURE: FLIMSY MONEY MINDED

As reported in the newspapers, a global financial rating agency last year conducted a survey across the 140 nations to ascertain financial literacy of its citizens. Individuals were tested on four basic financial concepts: Numeracy, Risk Diversification, Inflation and Compound Interest (Savings and Debt). The one who answered three question out of four correctly was considered financially literate. In general terms, financial literacy means our ability to understand how money works in the world and make an informed and judicious decision with regards to all the financial activities.

Results from India were astonishing. It was found out that close to 76% Indian adults do not adequately understand key financial concepts. It is widely known that India had almost 30% of the global wealth generation or GDP till 11th Century. It went on reducing in steps due to different reasons like social changes, political turmoil and aggressions from outsiders. In 18th century, India was at 24%, In 1820 AD 16%, 1870 – 12%, 1913 – 7.5%, 1950 – 4%, 1980 – 3%, 2008 – 5.5%.

Historical indian approach to money:

Just to make it very clear, I am not a financial superstar with multiple blockbusters to my credit. I am just a professional, who has paid heavy price for the financial illiteracy in my career. I sincerely do not want others to face similar roadblocks in their journey towards achieving their cherished dreams.

Historically we have approached money as a Necessary Evil which should be avoided as much as possible. Our ancient culture is based on "Being happy and content with whatever we have". These teachings were primarily aimed at educating people to have a balanced view of life and not count human life and its success or failure in terms of accumulated Wealth alone. Human tendency is to earn and accumulate a lot of wealth. People started taking whatever means possible to accumulate wealth. Scholars in the society had to take corrective measures of educating people about accumulating wealth by practicing socially accepted norms of making and growing money. Objective was to make people understand that there is no end to the greed for money and hence exploiting others to earn more and more wealth is not socially acceptable. Norms which were socially unacceptable were listed under SINS category whereas socially acceptable norms which were empowering fellow citizens were categorized under VIRTUES.

Throughout our ancient history barring last 300-400 years, Virtuous citizens were respected in the society and were awarded with Social status and prestigious, socially responsible leadership positions. These virtuous leaders were guiding our nation on the path of socially responsible attitudes and mutual growth. Barter system was prevalent for a long time. Wealth was measured necessarily by the material possessions like livestock e.g. Cows, bulls, Horses, elephants, goats or land etc.

The most basic fact of life is that as a human being, whatever we earn or accumulate in our lifetime is not transferable. It cannot be transferred to next life. It cannot be carried along on the onward journey after death. Understanding of this simple fact and our deep spiritual roots, have helped our flourishing nation stay grounded for ages.

We had a very strong and well evolved education system in place for centuries. Most of the life skills along with relevant specializations were taught in these schools in a very scientific manner.

We had internal skirmishes throughout our history but major damage or changes in this system were never forced upon us because the aggressors and losers were following the same culture and life style for ages.

With the advent of intense military aggressions by outsiders over the period especially in the last 400 odd years, our strongest backbone i.e. Fabled Education System and Deeply Spiritual Society were very systematically destroyed and broken down to pieces.

New rulers made us believe that our way of life was very primitive and unsophisticated. They brought their own education systems, belief systems and values to us. They made us follow their education systems, values and belief systems. Unfortunately they were successful in destroying our education system of employability and replaced it with Education system which could satiate their need for cheap and skilled labor.

Fortunately our spiritual belief systems are not yet completely broken.

The biggest change happening in society now is in terms of respect and authority accorded to people. Now we are giving respect to people with huge amounts of money whereas people with virtue and no money are left to fend for themselves. Virtuous leaders are extinct species whereas leaders with moneybags are ruling the roost. Young impressionable minds are following in their steps. Mindless pursuit of money is creating problems of epidemic proportions, rat race is one of the prominent among the lethal ones.

That is exactly why, we need to reskill ourselves with THE CURIOUS CASE OF MONEY.

The curious case of money

In the last 100 odd years, we have gone through a variety of cultural and economic changes. After independence, we got an excellent opportunity of detoxifying ourselves. The process was extremely slow in the beginning, but we are gathering momentum as we speak. Our definition of wealth changed from Knowledge, excellence and quality of life to money and material possessions. We are mindlessly pursuing money making at the cost of Health and quality of life. A large section of society is still poor and is struggling to survive every day. The aspirational middle class is working extremely hard for earning more and more money. Rural folks are looking for job opportunities in city centers. A lot of upheavals are taking place across the social layers. The most common thing is about earning and growing money.

Peer pressure is putting enormous influence on the decisions we are making in our day to day lives. Spending mindless amount of money on purchasing social status has become a fad.

Social security is getting tagged with the amount of money we possess. Social and electronic/ print media is perpetuating the Consumerism myth. There is a continuous competition to buy bigger and smarter TV or a bigger Car or the latest Smartphone.

Going by the advertisements in the media, finding a happy person without shiny new mobile or a fast car or social network following is a myth. Such happy person does not exist. Only way to lead a happy life is to buy as many gadgets or consumer products as possible. This mad race is forcing people to live beyond their means. They are falling in the debt trap of "Buy Now, Pay Later".

At the same time, we are neglecting the personal growth of ourselves and our families. We are focusing on developing our virtual image in the society or workplace instead of working on our real image and character.

On an emotional level, we are failing to detach ourselves from Money Syndrome. We are directly associating money with Pain and Pleasure. This direct association of Money with human feelings of pain and pleasure are inviting unnecessary attention of Mr. Cortisol and downward spiral is beginning from there. We are handing over the powers of deciding our wellbeing in the hands of Mr. Money. Sitting on a huge stash of money is pleasurable whereas having no money in the pocket is getting more and more painful.

Why are financial literacy and education so important?

Financial literacy is a very important life skill which can have wide repercussion on the decisions we make. Financial Literacy is utilizing knowledge of earning money, making right decisions to keep increasing the income and making the money work for you. It impacts the daily decisions an average family makes while trying to balance income and expenses.

Lack of financial literacy is a lifestyle disease caused by acute ignorance and carelessness developed due to overconfidence and lack of awareness. Financial illiteracy is not limited to developing or developed nations. It is a universal phenomenon. The level of financial literacy varies according to education and income levels. It is very common to find highly educated individuals with high incomes to be equally ignorant about financial issues.

Market forces and financial pressures are pushing individuals to think about learning financial basics. Day by day, the cost of making mistakes while making financial decisions is increasing exponentially.

Most worrisome part of the financial illiteracy is that most of us believe that we are far more financially literate than we really are. It makes us live in make belief world. Since we are not accepting the problem, there is no question of taking corrective measures to resolve it.

Any improvement in financial literacy will have a profound impact on our ability to provide for our future while avoiding the debt traps.

The cost of poor financial literacy?

Financial Literacy is one of the most important life skill, but that doesn't mean that people are rushing to improve their knowledge of all things related to money. Due to various reasons more and more people are becoming less and less financially literate as the years go by, and their lack of financial knowledge is costing them and their families dearly. Lack of financial literacy among all the sections of the society is directly affecting our economy.

Wrong financial decisions taken because of financial illiteracy are causing huge amount of loss in terms of resources like time, energy and money along with wastage of human productivity.

On the other hand financial institutes are taking advantage of customer's ignorance by making easy money available in terms of credit. These institutes are finding it extremely easy to lure ignorant clients by enticing them with various debt/loan schemes. Young salaried class typically makes wrong decisions right at the start of their careers based on malicious advice from their friends or colleagues or finance experts. Once we get into this debt trap, all our energy and time gets utilized in paying monthly installments. Majority of people spent more than they make. Most of us do not have any emergency savings. Situation is worrisome. More than half of working professionals fail to provision for monthly savings or emergency savings.

With large scale employment generation and academic qualifications, a lot of people are earning handsome salaries. We are extremely confident and proficient at making money. Once the basic needs are met, we start thinking about investing in assets or other financial tools. Once we start looking for options of safe investment, we immediately understand that we do not have the necessary knowledge of making investment decisions. Financial Services industry comes to our help, suggesting some fantastic investment options to choose from. By doing so, we end up shifting our responsibility to a professional at a fee. To begin with, we need to be financially literate enough to have a meaningful discussion with the financial advisor.

Way less than half of our population has sufficient understanding of the basic ideas necessary for successful financial planning. Improving financial condition of an individual or a family is creating a false sense of security. The lack of financial education is supplemented by lack of knowledgeable people who can impart these basic life skill trainings to people at the early stages of their careers.

Financial stress can affect nearly every facet of our life. If we constantly find ourselves consumed with the money we have (Or don't have), and how we are going to keep a roof over our head or how we are going to get to work and feed our family then we could certainly develop one of several stress-related health conditions. If these conditions are ignored or untreated it could often result in very serious, sometimes life-threatening illnesses.

Ignoring our finances to avoid finance related stress is not an option. In fact, tackling finance related issues head-on with the proper help of a guide or by self-study can be a better option. Being concerned about our finances is a good sign. Critical aspect is to handle it with proper knowledge and due diligence while keeping the stress causing situations under control. We should be able to recognize the point at which worrying about our finances results into stress build up in unhealthy way. It is time to stop and step back a little.

Financial stress and our health

Financial stress affects our health in many ways, these health issues can affect our personal, work and social life. Two of the most common effects of financial stress are anxiety and depression. These two conditions usually go hand-in-hand. The stress of having too much credit card debt, loan payments or medical bills can cause severe anxiety and depression. The feeling of being left behind financially or feeling of discouragement or feeling of hopelessness or feeling of constant worry are signs of one of the above unhealthy conditions.

Anxiety can manifest in many ways, but most people that suffer with it report panic attacks where our chest feels like its tightening, it becomes difficult to breathe, and it's often coupled with the inescapable sense of impending doom, the idea that something terrible is happening, it's growing, and it won't go away. Anxiety is mental as well as physical. Even if we aren't in the throes of a panic attack, we may still be experiencing racing and unwanted thoughts, profuse sweating, trembling, nausea, and a rapid heartbeat.

Depression goes beyond general feelings of sadness and self-doubt. Typical symptoms associated with depression are trouble sleeping, change in appetite (over eating or undereating), a lack of interest in favorite activities, taking unnecessary risks, particularly dark thoughts. Depression should not be taken lightly, since it is a response to stress caused by personal or financial problems.

We need to understand that Stress is an inherent physiologic response to a threat. When we're extremely stressed, our body enters the "fight or flight" mode. Adrenaline (a hormone that increases heart rate, pulse, and blood pressure) races through our veins during a stress reaction and we either want to utilize this adrenaline to 'fight' through the current situation or take 'flight' by running away, or avoiding the situation as much as possible. Physical responses occur inside our body when we're stressed, regardless of the cause. They can drastically affect our body and lead to severe health issues even if we're not aware of it. Pay attention to what our body is telling us.

When we are under stress, our body experiences immediate short-term effects, such as release of Cortisol, memory and concentration suppression, increased heart rate and blood pressure, faster breathing and reduction in metabolism. In the long-term, stress can increase the risk of Heart disease, stroke, digestive problems. It can lead to unhealthy weight gain or loss, skin problems, sleep issues etc.

Whether we are employed or unemployed, financial stress is a very common health condition. It is present across all the income groups irrespective of work profiles or educational qualifications.

Personal finance issues remains to be the leading cause of the stress followed closely by personal/family issues. Unfortunately personal finance issues are not specific to any age group. All the age groups from 18-25, 25-35, 35-45, 45-55 and 55-65 are victims of these stress causing issues.

Other conditions that can be caused or worsened by financial stress are Heart Disease/Attack, Gastrointestinal Problems,

Weight Gain/Loss, Eating Disorders, Diabetes, Insomnia, Psoriasis, Cancer, High Blood Pressure and Substance Abuse etc.

Preventing stress-related illnesses?

First step in preventing stress related illnesses is to understand that we can do something about the situation which is creating the stress. All of us face stressful situations some or the other time, but the way in which we react to the situations or issues makes all the difference. For instance, let's say that you have started a new business and suddenly you suffer a major health problem. Allowing yourself to succumb to the symptoms of financial or personal stress could cause depression, anxiety and other complications. You will be able to overcome the situation faster if you can focus and take properly planned actions to get out of the situation.

TIPS FOR STRESS RELIEF:

Consult Your Doctor

Do something relaxing

Spend time with family and friends

Spend time pursuing a hobby

Listen to music

Read

Do something spiritual

Focus on the positives

Watch favorite movies or television shows

Consciously avoid stressful people & situations

Deep Breathing

Meditation

Eat a healthy snack

Yoga

Exercise

Better yet, be proactive. Consult the source of the stress, and spend some of your time working towards changing that. Write a budget and get your finances down on paper. See what you make, what your monthly responsibilities are, and what your debts are. Even getting it all on the page will help you confront it. Take small steps. Make the budget, and take a break before you come back to tally up the totals. Once you do get some numbers down, don't panic! Remember, your health is your most valuable asset.

Readiness for a financial crisis?

A large amount of debt, a job loss or overtime reduction, medical bills, or simply being irresponsible with our spending could cause undue financial stress. We call each of these instances a financial crisis. Even if we are financially responsible, an unexpected expense could be all it takes to send us into financial duress, especially if we're not prepared to cope with it.

A financial crisis is very difficult to plan for, and unless we've created a budget for a crisis in advance, we could find ourselves in a very unpleasant situation. It all spirals down from there.

Why should financial literacy be taught in schools?

We cannot deny the fact that the financial literacy is "A Must Have Life Skill", but does this mean that schools should be responsible for educating students about financial literacy? Improving financial literacy levels in our society is not the responsibility of an institute or organization alone. This task is beyond the capacity of any single organization. It will need a uniform response from all the stakeholders in the society. Financial Literacy improvement cannot be a onetime activity, it has to be a continuous lifelong process. While we agree with the fact that the schools cannot have the sole responsibility of developing and improving financial literacy, but schools certainly are the best placed institutes to play a very important role in this process.

We can very easily ascertain the fact that the most successful people in financial matters have an exposure to financial management very early in their lives. Including financial education in our primary and secondary school years can provide a very solid foundation for financial literacy buildup. This will help younger people avoid poor financial decisions and its consequences which can take years to overcome.

Without being judgmental about the school teachers and authorities, we need to enhance their capacity to cover financial literacy topics by empowering them with trainings, infrastructure and resources. Some schools are covering certain aspects of financial literacy which needs to be appreciated wholeheartedly.

How can we teach financial literacy in schools?

We are very aware of the fact that some education experts are of the opinion that the current curricula are already full of multiple subjects and disciplines. We must make sure that the financial literacy topic gets included in the curriculum. It will help in development of skills, knowledge and attitudes necessary for sound financial literacy. We cannot afford to shield our young generation anymore from this topic. We'll be doing injustice to the younger generation by not equipping them with a very potent life skill. Many schools are already teaching areas of financial literacy, however the lack of resources and training in this field means it is difficult to teach in any depth or in a coordinated manner.

How can we educate our kids about finance?

In an effort to train the next generation to make better personal financial decisions, schools are starting to address financial education in their curriculum. While some children are still growing up making the same mistakes their parents made. It is very common for a youngster to spend more than he earns each month. Real life application of financial concepts and healthy money habits must start at home and then should be taught in the schools.

As a parent, we can help our child avoid this scenario later in life by teaching a few core principles in the right way. Here are some of the basics of finance for kids that we can work on at home.

It's never too early to start

It is found that our money habits may be formed as early as age seven. Not only that, but some researchers say that even toddlers can comprehend the very basic concepts of saving. Why not go with our child to open his first savings account when they are young? This way we can teach our sons or daughters how to save first and spend what is left. This is a great and simple exercise that helps our child start a lifelong healthy financial habit.

If we want something, sometimes it's better to wait!

Delaying gratification is a useful skill in almost any role in life, and has even been linked to overall success in adulthood. It is a general life concept that holds true in financial scenarios too.

Having goals in any area of life works,

Not just finances, but in money matters it's particularly useful and effective. An idea for a child's goal might be a new toy. We'll probably have to set up a daily or weekly or monthly pocket money for our child so he or she has a way to reach the goal. Let us have them add money to the pot and monitor their progress towards the goal.

Discipline about timelines is also a very critical tool

The sooner we start taking care of our finances, the larger the reward we'll reap later on.

Explaining the concepts immediately followed up by practical application of them in the real life helps children understand the concept in a better way. Some of us have apprehensions about teaching children financial literacy so early in their lives, in our opinion, students tend to forget about it since immediate need of applying these concepts is not there. Though this is a valid point to a certain extent, the cost of not teaching children about financial literacy early in their life, overweighs the benefits of not teaching them these skills. We will have to keep them nudging with different concepts and their real life applications. Financial education cannot be treated as a one-time certification exam, but a lifelong continuous process.

Most of us very conveniently tend to think that giving children money is the easiest way of teaching them about it. It is simply not true. We cannot act like an ATM (All-time Money) for our children. When we buy something our child requests, be it an ice cream or a toy, where does the money come from? Are our children getting a feeling that the money just came out of our pockets magically? Similarly when we are withdrawing money from ATMs in front of our children, are they getting an impression that money just comes out of ATM boxes automatically and anybody can go to the ATM and withdraw money. We need to explain it to them, how money reached these ATM boxes in the first place and why do they allow us to withdraw certain amount.

Without making it sound like a complex task, we can turn simple daily/weekly or monthly shopping routines into important lessons about finance management. Before leaving home for shopping for groceries or household items, we can spend some time with our child making him prepare a list of items we need to purchase under the pre-decided amount of money. We can incentivize them by allowing them to keep the balance money in their Money Bank pot or in their own Savings account. This can be a simple way of explaining them proper use of money with an immediate reward at the end of the activity. Simple tasks like these can inculcate the true meaning of financial concepts on their minds.

We can associate happiness and enjoyment with collecting or saving or earning a reward money. If our child does well in the sports activity or in a school test, we can appreciate his/ her efforts and celebrate this little success by having an ice cream or doing some activity together which both of us will enjoy. It does not necessarily have to be a reward in terms of handing over money to the child. Child will associate earning the reward in terms of money buying ice cream or two movie tickets with achieving certain objective in a school or in personal space.

On the similar lines, we can simulate a typical loan scenario with our child. Let us say our child wants a full cricket gear. We can explain the concept of loans by offering him a loan. We can do this in a proper bank style by explaining him the terms of Interest and repayment schedule with penalty charges against non-payment of installments. Penalty can be charged in terms of doing some additional household stuff like washing the car or something like it. Important part of this activity is to make him understand whether he needs to take a loan for buying something and how he is going to pay for it. This simple task has the potential of liberating the child from the worldly trap of "Buy Now, Pay Later".

Children have the most impressionable minds. They observe and learn from the people around them. If we are reacting to financial matters negatively, they will also pick up those habits subconsciously. If we are reacting angrily to bank statements or utility bills in front of our children, they will presume that these financial matters are annoying and should be avoided. If we are throwing our bills or statements away unopened, we are basically telling our children that these are nuisances which should be avoided.

It is a better idea to allow our children participate in some of the household purchase decisions. Let them express their views on better options of buying things or about saving money. We may be surprised with their inputs.

I was surprised by a question my daughter once asked me. She asked me, if money doesn't grow on trees, why Money Plants are called so?

In my opinion, buying school stationery can play a very important role in educating the child about financial concepts. Buying school stationery is all around the year process. We can allocate certain amount for school stationery every month and let the child decide about spending and saving from the budget. This will make him participate in the process with responsibility.

I had a savings bank account when I was in the 5th standard. I used to deposit scholarship amount in this bank account. My grandmother used to accompany me for these bank visits. We can get a savings account opened for our child. We can explain him the purpose of the account. It is necessary to open account in her name and opt for bank statement by mail. Let the child open the envelope containing the bank statement with her name written on it. Explain her how the balance grows and interest gets added. Arrange for a separate folder for her monthly statements and the cheque book, if any. These things will make her aware of the organized record keeping and easy tracing of the account status.

Online banking is ok. But taking child to the bank branch and make her deposit and withdraw money using Deposit and withdrawal slips is a fantastic way of financial education plus personal bonding. Indian government's demonetization drive was a good opportunity of taking children to banks and explaining those banking operations.

Explaining investment options to grow our money quickly is next step. We can start explaining multiple investment options like stock market, real estate, Entrepreneurship etc. Most teenagers can understand basics of stocks and trading. Potential risks and rewards of investing in the stock market can be explained in detail. Simulation techniques can be used to practice trading without actually buying or selling the stocks. My friend used to do this while training his students. He used to allocate a certain amount of virtual money to everybody. Then these students used to study different stocks and their performances. Based on their understanding of the market trends and company performances, they used to sell and buy different stocks by noting them on their notepads. The actual performance can be judged after a stipulated time period of let us say week or a month without investing any real money. Once the students started performing consistently over a period of time, they were allowed to trade on the real trading platforms.

There is a very realistic chance of losing money due to whatever reasons but the idea is to take well informed decisions after considering all the worst case scenarios.

Statements for all the finance related documents should be addressed to the child. These documents should get filed in the folder properly.

We need to keep in mind an old saying about teaching a man to fish and feeding him for a lifetime versus giving him a fish to feed him for a day. These early exercises in money management will teach our children valuable financial lessons to last him or her well into adulthood. Many parents invest large sums of money on behalf of their children. Similarly, educating children about handling his or her financial affairs is an equally important responsibility. In the long run, teaching children about money will be more valuable than giving them money and no direction on how to handle it.

Vacation time!

Vacations typically mean a lot of spare time for children to try and learn new things like hobbies, sports and entertainment. Child may be looking for a bicycle or a pair of cool running shoes. We should encourage him to see beyond impulse purchases by separating "Spending Now" and "Saving for the big purchase" in the near future.

I always like the process of buying a new car. What we typically do is after sufficient online research of different car models and reading their launch reviews, long term user reviews, we shortlist 2-3 models. We visit multiple showrooms or websites to compare the prices and offers. Collecting car brochures is a big time pass for kids. If children also can join us in shortlisting these cars, collecting estimates and offers, taking test-drives, they can give their feedback which can help us select the best car. In the process, children also learn the process of comparing different products for the performance, quality, cost and usability. Overall, it becomes a bargain shopping tutorial for them.

Things to avoid

With best of our intentions to educate our child about financial concepts, sometimes we make some very simple mistakes.

The most common mistake that most of us make is to keep children away from money related matters or discussions. It sends the message that either money is not important or it's something which should be feared and never mentioned like Lord Voldemort in Harry Potter Series. If we are not going to discuss these things with children, obvious default options are school and the media. We have discussed schools in details. If children end up learning financial concepts from the media, then they are the readymade "Forever Credit card Soldiers" of the new economy.

Second mistake we make is to discuss financial matters openly only when things are going well. It is far better to be honest about problems like bad decisions or bounced cheque or pending bills etc. Most basic reason behind these problems creating enormous stress and discomfort is our reluctance to look at it like a typical problem. We tend to never treat finance related issues like any other problems in our life. Applying different yardsticks of secrecy and confidentiality to these problems turns them into silent killers. Accepting them as problems is the first step. Problems can be challenging but there are always various ways and means to tackle them.

Third common mistake is related to age old wisdom that the "Money doesn't Grow on Trees". All of us must have heard about it at some point in time. There is nothing wrong with the logic. All of us have a natural tendency of giving kids money so that they can enjoy their childhood and we don't feel guilty of not being able to fulfill their wishes. These two aspects are self-contradictory. On the one hand we are saying money doesn't grow on trees which means it is hard to earn the money. On the other hand we are giving them easy money. Children get confused and the financial lesson is lost. We can have a common understanding with our children that they will get money if they will finish certain simple tasks beyond their regular responsibilities like cleaning a room in the house. Small gifts of cash can be understandable if they are communicated properly. Children should not get the feeling of entitlement.

The next false assumption we make is to consider financial concepts too heavy for children to learn so early in their life. Young generation is extremely tech savvy and their grasping powers are really good. They are exposed to so much technology and awareness, that these basic concepts can be very easily taught to them at a very young age. The communication needs to be adjusted to their understanding levels. Let characters from cartoon series like Doramon help them understand these basics.

Most important precaution we can take is to practice what we preach. If we are not practicing the basics of financial management, our children will follow us in the same way. Any number of words without conforming actions will yield no results.

Passing on the baton!

We are busy earning money and making sure that our family does not face any hardships related to money issues. In the process of earning the money and fulfilling their every wish, we are hampering their own life skill development by making them dependent on us for everything. Passing on the money to the next generation without imparting proper understanding of its usage is a recipe for disaster. Instilling right values can be more fruitful in the long run.

We are concentrating on building up assets for our children, if we fail to impart right set of values and skill sets to manage or grow these assets, our next generation can very easily squander away everything we had built for them.

Children will learn by watching us. If we can showcase simple facts that we are working hard, we are earning money, we are saving some of it and are not spending on unimportant things, our children will also follow the same.

Gifts and Instant gratification with debt are the most common reasons of financial illiteracy epidemic. Receiving gifts frequently without any reasons prevents the child from appreciating the value of the gifts. Extended logic of gift can be inheritance or the family business. When the inheritance or family business is passed down to children, they fail to understand and appreciate the value. Teaching children to avoid buying something in the spur of the moment makes them understand the importance of waiting. It also helps them avoid instant gratification trap.

Learning money management skills takes time. We are still learning them. Children will make many mistakes while learning them. We should encourage them to correct these mistakes instead of us jumping right into it. Let them make mistakes and learn to correct them. It will boost their confidence. They will learn that everything costs money and their decisions related to money have consequences.

It is very clear that we are focusing on Kids for improving the Financial Literacy.

Kids first

Literacy is the ability to read and write. It is a fundamental part of the education system. Many adults avoid talking to kids about money because they lack confidence in how they've handled their own finances. It is a wasted opportunity. Even after making so many mistakes in managing finance, adults have experience and perspective which kids do not.

What exactly money is?

Let us try and understand what exactly money is and how it ends up in our wallet.

Barter

Before money was used as a common medium of exchanging goods and services, people used to barter or trade with each other. They used to exchange things with each other. Items such as fruits, food grains, seashells were used for barter. Depending on the availability and the quality of the item, people used to mutually agree upon exchange rates. E.g. 5 kg rice can be exchanged with 3 kg wheat. Scarce the material, greater the value.

Bartering system survived for a long time. There were some practical limitations of this system. For typical bartering transaction, items used to be carried to a common point where actual exchange used to take place. Carrying all the items everywhere was not easy. Since it was very difficult to divide some of the components equally, most of the times division used to be left to discretion of the individuals.

Since bartering was difficult, people needed an easier way to buy or exchange the things they required. Systems like seashells, or beads or coins solved many of these problems. They were easy to carry, divide and were sturdy enough to survive for a long time.

Money

Money is used to pay for everything. Currently we have two forms of money: Coins and currency notes. Coins are made of metal whereas notes are printed on paper. Coins and Notes have various sizes and are worth a certain amount of money.

In India, we have Indian Rupee Notes and coins available in the market. Various sizes of coins are 25 Paise. 50 Paise, 1 Rupee, 2 Rupee, 5 Rupee and 10 Rupee. Currency notes available are 5 Rs, 10 Rs, 20 Rs, 50 Rs, 100 Rs, 500 Rs, 1000 Rs and 2000 Rs.

There are a number of ways in which we can help children identify and play with various coins and currency notes:

Giving children a certain amount of coins and guiding them to sort different coins in separate groups.

Once the coins are separated, we can explain each type of coin and its worth.

We can explain various combinations of coins to prepare a set amount of money. e.g. We can ask children to create a 100 rupee stack by using different coins.

We can explain worth of each coin by giving real life examples. Like we can buy a Chocolate by paying 20 rupees.

We can show and explain various notes and their values.

We can ask children to prepare some odd number of amount by using notes and coins. e.g. For making a payment of 356 rupees, children will have to get 3 100 rupee notes, one fifty rupee note, one 5 rupee coin and single one rupee coin.

After practicing, let us make our kid count the coins and notes to pay for a small purchase at the candy store.

We need to explain various other methods of payment like credit cards, NetBanking and cheques. Though these are more complex methods of payment.

Earning money

Kids can observe that the money comes from our wallet and the ATM machine, but they may not be aware that the money has to be earned first. We need to explain that most adults get a job so that they can earn money, called income. A certain amount of money earned by doing a job is Salary.

We can explain about our job and how we get paid. E.g. "I work at a factory. I get paid every weekend. Our family uses this money to pay for grocery, clothes and transport. We save some money for our planned purchase of bike."

Most kids like to talk about the job they would like to do when they grow up. We can build on this topic by asking relevant questions.

We can try and make children think about their favorite subjects in school?

Why they like those subjects?

What are typical jobs related to these subjects?

What are your favorite hobbies?

Is it possible to point out jobs which can use these hobbies as skills?

Many parents will be excited to hear these things, but it's important to encourage children to think freely based on relevant questions. Killing their enthusiasm by asking negative questions or by making negative comments is not a good idea. Listen, discuss and allow them to draw their own conclusions.

Pocket money

Giving a certain pocket money every week can be a good idea. Since kids have very little opportunity to earn money, pocket money gives them an opportunity to practice saving and making good spending choices. Birthdays are a great time to increase the pocket money amount.

Chores can be associated with pocket money. Children can be taught that finishing certain activity will earn them the pocket money. It makes the kids observe the relationship between working and getting paid. Importantly we must make sure that children do take some responsibility of some tasks which are their primary tasks. Pocket money cannot be related to primary tasks. Any tasks finished by children over and above their primary tasks can be associated with Pocket money.

Goods and services

Goods and Services are the most basic ideas to be learnt. For understanding of the kids, we use money to buy both goods and services. Goods are basically objects that can be bought. Whereas Services are actions performed with specific intention.

Goods

These are the things that are made or grown and something that we can use or consume. To simplify for kids, we can say that goods are the things that can be touched. We should ask child to have a look around and name few goods items. Some of the examples of goods are balls, tables, football, plates, TV, books etc. Goods are things that people buy to use one time (e.g. candy) or over and over (e.g. Cricket bat). Some goods are manufactured or made e.g. cars, balls. Other goods are grown, including fruits and vegetables.

Services

Service is a work that somebody does for others. Service is an action. Examples of services that can be found around are Teachers, Doctors, Engineers, lawyers, drivers etc.

Services can be private or public. Public services are typically paid by the government. Whereas other services paid by individuals can be dentists, farmers, nurses etc.

There can be a combination of goods and services. Some services end up into goods. One such example can be a service of cooking food that people buy and eat (goods). Similarly farmers provide the service of sowing and harvesting the food that people purchase and consume.

Needs and wants

Needs and Wants are an important concept for kids to understand. Needs are things that we must have in order to survive. Wants, on the other hand, are things that we would like to have, but that are not necessary for survival. Some needs and wants don't cost any money. Whereas many needs and wants, cost money.

Needs include basic utilities, transportation, food, shelter, medical care etc. Examples of wants include movies, television, Toys etc.

Most people earn money from their jobs so that they can pay for the things they need and some of the things they want. We need to explain the difference between needs and wants so kids can spend money wisely. We can ask kids to answer some of the questions like, what will happen if we spent entire salary on toys for one week, with nothing left for food or other expenses. We need to explain why we have to pay for the needs first and then opt for wants, if possible.

Differentiating between needs and wants is the critical aspect. Sometimes the same thing can be a need or a want depending on the utilization or purpose of the usage or consumption. Buying a car in order to drop kids to school, get to work, go to the grocery store is a need. Whereas luxurious and bigger car is a want.

Food category has needs such as fruits, vegetables, grains etc. These are needs of the body for its nourishment. Sodas, Ice creams are examples of wants.

Kids just need to understand that there is a finite supply of money to pay for the goods and services that your family needs or wants.

Spending choices

We have to constantly make choices about what to read, what to wear at party, which car to buy etc. Everybody including children have to make different choices daily. We have to make simple decisions.

Part of making good spending choices is being aware of the difference between needs and wants. The adults in the house will pay for the needs such as food and transportation. After all the needs are taken care of, the family might have some money left over for wants. We can ask kids to take a decision about whether they want to go ahead and spend on wants.

As the kids grow, they can select from more alternatives. We can ask kids to prepare a list of their needs and a separate list of their wants.

Asking child to choose single important item from the list can be very difficult for him. He may really want all the items on the list. To help child make a choice, ask him or her to think about each item, listing reasons to buy each item and reasons not to buy each item. If deciding about a video game, for example, child might come up with something like:

Reasons to buy - my friends have it; I like it

Reasons not to buy - I can play it at my friend's house; I have a lot of video games already; it costs a lot of money

Helping child eliminate some of the wants from the list by using this process, until the list is down to a manageable number of items is a better option. Kids tend to make the best choices if their own money is involved.

We can encourage good spending choices by asking questions such as, "Do I need to buy this now? Would this cost less somewhere else? Can I borrow this from the library or from a friend?" We can also include children in some of our small spending decisions. At the grocery store, for example, you might explain why you chose one brand over another. You could say, "This toothpaste is INR 55 and the other one is only INR 45. They both look the same. Which one do you think we should buy?"

If the child knows that we are putting a lot of thought into each spending choice, he or she may be more likely to do the same. If our child is using his or her own money, we can help him or her evaluate the choices.

Saving

Most kids associate the accumulation of coins in their piggy banks with the concept of saving. For some goals, we don't have to save for very long before we have enough money. These are called short-term goals. On the other hand, elder children will have long-term goals to save for bigger things such as cars and college.

It can be difficult for some kids to wait before buying something they want, but this is an important lesson to learn. It may be helpful to discuss other times when our child must wait for something he or she wants: standing in line for a turn on the playground, waiting for his or her favorite vacation or a planned family holiday.

If our child really wants a certain toy (or anything) but does not have enough money to buy it, explain that he or she can save their money in a safe place, such as a piggy bank or jar, until he or she has saved enough to pay for the item. Help him or her create a mini-budget for the purchase and figure out: How much he or she has saved already

How much the item will cost (including tax)?

How much money he or she expects to "earn" each week?

How long it will take to save?

Resist the temptation to step in and help your child pay for the last few dollars. It diminishes your child's efforts and any feelings of accomplishment he or she could have by reaching the goal on his or her own.

Many children, for example, really like a particular toy and decide to get it. Over the period of time though they may decide that toy is not so important after all. Waiting to make a purchase is an excellent way of avoiding impulse buying and is an effective tool for helping kids determine what they really want and what they can do without.

Saving accounts

Many banks have savings accounts designed especially for kids, with no minimum deposit amounts and no minimum balance requirements.

While the interest rates these days may not do much to encourage kids to save, most kids will nevertheless like the idea that their money can earn more money. Younger children may not understand the mathematics behind interest or the idea of compounding just yet, but they are old enough to appreciate the fact that their money can earn interest.

The monthly statements, passbook gets kids excited, and since most of today's kids are tech-savvy, reviewing account balances online can be easy. Watching their account grow over time can encourage even very young children to save and to make wise spending choices. We can add money to our savings account (called a deposit) and can take money out when we need it (a withdrawal). The bank helps us keep track of our money by sending out statements in the mail or via email.

Less financially literate people tend to accumulate less wealth, borrow more and are less likely to invest or know the terms of their mortgages or other loans. People with a high degree of financial literacy, on the other hand, are more likely to make plans for retirement, and those who do plan for retirement have more than twice the wealth of people who do not plan.

Money is an exciting topic for kids, and many are eager to learn about earning, spending and saving money, even at a very young age. Most young children are ready to learn the basic concepts introduced here: what money is, goods and services, needs and wants, spending choices and savings goals. Keep in mind, however, that much of this learning is the result of repetition, experience and practice.

Now let us focus on teens:

We have covered some basic concepts for kids like income and expenses, needs and wants etc. Let us learn some more advanced topic suitable for teenagers, like budgeting, credit and debt, money management and investing.

Taxes

Teenage students can understand slightly complex issues in a better way. We need to explain that people earn money for working. They don't get all the money they earned. Some of the earnings go to the central and state governments as taxes that will be used to pay for roads, public schools, governance and other such programs.

Budgeting

Budget is an estimation of income and expenses that can be used to plan spending as per the priority of the tasks while arranging for the necessary money i.e. cash flow. Budget is a financial tool that can help us:

Plan for expenses

Budget helps us note prepare a list of anticipated immediate, short-term and long-term expenses. Short-term expenses are expected to happen in the coming month; mid-term expenses are expected in between one month and a year; long-term expenses are expected after a year.

Cut spending

Budget helps us get a very clear understanding of areas in which we are spending the money. Depending on our understanding of criticality and importance of these work areas, we can reduce or increase funding allocated to certain tasks. We can make informed decisions on optimizing the spending patterns.

Spend wisely

Budget gives us clarity on the balance between income and expenses. If Income is more than the expenses, we can decide on better utilizing surplus money. If the expenses are more than income, we can take necessary actions for reducing the expenses and increasing the income.

Save for future goals

Budget helps us make provisions for expected expenses in the future.

Develop lifelong money management habits

It is priceless to learn as a teenager how to save for a goal. For most people, this is not as simple as setting aside a certain amount of money every month; it usually involves making intelligent spending choices, and preferring savings over wants.

Creating a budget

Let us prepare a budget by outlining income and expense statements based on realistic projections. Since estimates are based on previous income and expense patterns supported with knowledge of future projections, we can make children record all of their expenses. This kind of information for last two to three months can help children with readymade data to base their estimates on.

Like a typical school experiment scenario, we can use paper, pencil or computer program like Excel to create a budget. We need to always keep in mind that this subject is not a very colorful, happening subject. We need to make it as interesting and funny as possible.

Estimates: income and expense

A typical budget should include income projections and expense projections. Income projections should include all sources of income, such as:

Salary

Incentives or bonuses

Gifts

Interest and dividends

We can include either before tax or after tax estimates. In case of before tax estimates, we will have to add a separate column of taxes in expense category.

Budgeting for expenses needs to be made in detail. One Bills section in a budget will not help us with clear picture of where money is getting spent. We'll have to keep on updating various heads and in the future depending on the inclusions or exclusions of certain kind of expenses. Some of the typical expense items are:

Food – Snacks, Groceries

Car - loan payment, insurance, fuel, maintenance.

Entertainment – Books, movies, music, etc.

Personal - clothes, toiletries, haircuts, etc.

House Rent

Savings

Utilities Bills – maintenance fees, cell phone bills

Since we are making children prepare the budget, we can consider pocket money as their monthly or weekly income. If there are large variations in monthly income and expenses depending on seasonal expenses, we can create a separate budget for each month which can be consolidated after completing 12 months budgeting.

After noting down all of the income sources and all known expenses for needs, goods, services that we must pay for, we can consolidate these numbers. Typical budget created by children in excel might look like this:

Description		January	February	March	April	May	June	TOTAL
Income								
	Salary	$2,700	$2,700	$2,700	$2,700	$2,700	$2,700	$16,200
	Incentive	$200	$0	$0	$200	$200	$0	$600
	Gifts	$0	$75	$75	$0	$0	$0	$150
	Interest	$23	$23	$23	$23	$23	$23	$138
Income Total		$2,923	$2,798	$2,798	$2,923	$2,923	$2,723	$17,088
Expenses								
Personal	Clothes	$400	$0	$0	$0	$3,000	$0	$3,400
	Haircuts	$150	$150	$150	$150	$150	$150	$900
Bike	Cost	$2,900	$0	$0	$0	$0	$0	$2,900
	Maintenance	$0	$0	$0	$50	$75	$0	$125
Food	Groceries	$550	$480	$643	$500	$490	$600	$3,263
	Snacks	$75	$45	$125	$65	$83	$56	$449
Entertainment	movies	$120	$120	$120	$120	$120	$120	$720
	books	$250	$0	$0	$0	$0	$170	$420
	Picnic	$0	$0	$0	$0	$240	$0	$240
Utility bills	Cellphone	$300	$300	$300	$300	$300	$300	$1,800
Savings	Savings	$250	$250	$250	$250	$250	$250	$1,500
Expense Total		$4,995	$1,345	$1,588	$1,435	$4,708	$1,646	$15,717
Income-Expense		-$2,072	$1,453	$1,210	$1,488	-$1,785	$1,077	$1,371

In this example six months are shown to illustrate income and expense status from month to month. The last row highlighted in yellow shows, if the budget is balanced for the month. Here we can see that we have spent more than our income in two months.

Without this budget in front of them, children will not be able to understand of imagine how they are spending their money or where they can control their expenses.

Inflation

Inflation a steady increase in the price of goods and services over the period of fixed timeframe. It is usually measured in terms of a specific annual percentage which helps us in provisioning for protection buffer against the future risks safely.

We wonder why things cost more over period of time. Concept of inflation will help us understand the same. Inflation directly affects our buying power. Assuming that we are earning INR 50 per week, if inflation is at 3%, after one year we would need INR 51.50 to be able to purchase the same goods and services that last year's INR 50 could buy.

Inflation can help us better understand our favorite subject of salary increase. If I have a job, for salary increment to actually increase my buying power, percentage increase has to be more than the inflation percentage. For example, if inflation is 3%, any salary increase above 3% will effectively increase my buying power. If inflation rate and salary increase percentage is equal, there is no effective increase in my buying power. Inflation needs to be considered in budgeting. Many of the goods and services we are buying today may increase in price next year as a result of inflation. If we are planning to buy those goods and services again next year, we'll have to provision money with inflation in mind.

Credit and debt

These two concepts are the most important aspects which must be paid undivided attention to. Credit is the ability to borrow money. Money borrowed on credit is called Loan. Loan is a promise to pay the original amount back with a little extra (interest) within mutually agreed upon timeframe.

Maintaining Credit-worthiness is a very important financial tool. It is typically measured with a credit score. The most common credit score in India is CRISIL or CIBIL score. Having a good credit score helps in following financial transactions:

Borrow money

Get approval for a credit card

Rent an apartment or house

Qualify for a loans (home, personal, car etc)

Get better interest rates on credit cards and loans

Get better car insurance rates

Creditworthiness is typically measured with a credit score. The most common credit score is the CRISIL or CIBIL score. CRISIL Limited and Credit Information Bureau India Limited (CIBIL) with some more credit rating agencies help lenders evaluate the risks of extending credit or disbursing loan amounts to people based on their repayment capacity and discipline.

Lenders typically review the Four Cs when making a decision to grant a loan:

Capacity - your present and future ability to meet your payment obligations

Capital - the value of your assets and your net worth

Character - your payment history

Collateral - the property or assets that will secure the loan

When evaluating the Four Cs, the loan officer may ask you questions such as:

Are you employed? How much money do you earn each month?

What are your monthly expenses?

How much money do you have in bank accounts?

Have you had credit in the past?

How many credit cards do you have?

What collateral can you offer?

You can be denied a loan if you are unable to demonstrate that you have capacity, capital, character and collateral. For example, you may get turned down if you have:

A history of making late payments

Filed for bankruptcy

Had property repossessed or foreclosed

A court order requiring you to pay money to a lender or creditor

Individual credit score affects one's ability to qualify for different types of credit and varying interest rates. In general, the higher the credit score, the better the loan terms like interest rates and tenure.

Even when all other factors remain the same, a younger person will likely have a lower credit score than an older person. That's because the length of a credit history accounts for 15% of the credit score. Your teen or young adult can be at a disadvantage simply because he or she does not have the depth or length of credit history.

Five factors are included and weighted to calculate a person's credit score:

35%: payment history

30%: amounts owed

15%: length of credit history

10%: new credit and recently opened accounts

10%: types of credit in use

About loans

There are two types of installment loans: secured loans and unsecured loans.

A **secured** installment loan is backed by collateral (something of value that the lender can take if you default on the loan). Because of the collateral, the interest rates for secured installment loans are comparatively lower than unsecured loans. A car loan is a secured installment loan: if you stop making payments, the lender can take the car from you and sell it to recover some of the money (you are still responsible for the difference between what you owe and how much the lender can get for the car).

An **unsecured** installment loan, on the other hand, is not backed by any collateral. Because this exposes the lender to more risk, the interest rates are comparatively higher than for secured loans. A student loan is a type of unsecured installment loan.

Investing

To grow your money, is the goal always. There are various means of investing the money. Keeping children educated about these different investment methods will certainly help them. Selection of right mode of investment depends largely on objective of the investment and risk appetite. Though objective is always about growing money, risk appetite can help us choose the right solution.

Risk appetite

Risk appetite is the amount of risk an individual can take on his or her investment. It is the point till which despite of losses he or she is ready to hold on to their investment. It also can be defined as the extent to which we are willing to risk our money to earn high profits. Generally, risk and rewards tends to have direct proportion. Higher the risk, greater the rewards.

Expectations drive our appetite for risk. If we are expecting to earn higher growth on the investment, we should be ready to take greater risks. Risk appetite is a very personal judgement. Some of us may be happy with 8% annual returns whereas rest of us may expect more than 10% annual returns on their investments. Our current financial position also guides our risk appetite. If we are financially very secure and can afford to wager our money in risky options even at some loss, our risk appetite is higher.

Investment options

Risky investments offer high or sometimes no returns, whereas safe investments offer steady but lower incomes. Generally speaking choosing an investment option which matches our return expectation and within our risk appetite comfort zone is a safe option.

Right investment option can be selected using three parameters which are Liquidity, Safety and Return potential. Liquidity is the ease of converting investment to cash. Safety refers to the level of the risk involved in the investment. Let us have a look at multiple investment options:

Banks – This type of investment option is the deposits and accounts in the banks. Banks offer saving accounts, recurring deposit accounts and fixed deposit accounts. Biggest advantage of these options is safety at lower returns and high liquidity.

Saving accounts are highly liquid but carry lower interest. These are suitable for day-today usage and emergencies. Fixed deposit carry slightly higher interest rates and can be used for short term or long term investment requirements. The recurring deposit schemes are for saving money every month.

Government Schemes – Government launches various schemes aimed at investments such as National Savings Certificates, Public Provident Funds, Post Office schemes etc.

Bonds – A bond is basically a loan given to the company by a buyer in return for interest. Bonds can be issued by companies, financial institutions or governments. The value of the bond is returned to the buyer on the maturity date plus the interest income. Bonds can be tax saving bonds or regular bonds.

Company Fixed deposits – These are fixed deposits issued by companies to attract small investors. They offer attractive interest rates and are payable only on maturity. Company fixed deposits are insecure. Their authenticity and security can be judged only by their ratings.

Debentures – These are similar to bonds but are issued by companies. Debentures can be of different kinds. Non-Convertible debentures (NCD) redeems total amount to the buyer. Partially Convertible debentures (PCD) redeems partial amount and remaining amount is converted to equity shares with or without the option to the investor. Fully convertible debentures (FCD) converts whole value into equity.

Mutual Funds – A mutual fund is an investment tool made up of a pool of funds collected from many investors for the purpose of investing in securities such as stocks, bonds or assets or some combination of these investments. Mutual funds are operated by fund managers who invest this capital to earn better returns. Various types of mutual funds are Equity funds (stocks), money market funds, fixed income funds (bonds). Mutual funds can be classified as open ended or closed ended, depending on the maturity date of the fund.

Equity Shares – A stock market is an open space for selling or buying company shares. The main stock exchanges in India are BSE (Bombay Stock Exchange) and NSE (National Stock Exchange). The purpose of a stock exchange is to facilitate the trading of shares.

Insurance Policies – Insurance policies are bought as a safety mechanism of insurance against future loss. The policies are Life Insurance or Term Insurance, Endowment policies, Money back policies etc.

Diversifying your investments

Don't put all your eggs in one basket is age old mantra. Diversification follow the similar logic of risk management by mixing a variety of high risk, low risk investments in one portfolio. Diversification is aimed at balancing riskier investments with safer investments to limit and control overall potential financial risk.

Assets and liabilities

Assets are everything that you own, and liabilities include everything that you owe. Assets are resources that are owned by an individual or entity. Assets are expected to generate benefit to the owner. Liabilities are obligations that makes an individual or entity transfer benefits including money, good or services to another individual or entity.

Interest (earning interest & paying interest)

Interest is a small increment in the money that a borrower needs to pay the lender along with the principal. Interest can be earned or interest can be paid depending on whether we are lending the money to borrowers or borrowing from lenders.

It can be explained using real life scenarios, we can earn interest when we loan money to the bank. If you have a savings account, for example, the bank pays you a small amount of money for depositing the money with them. The bank, incidentally, uses your money - that's why it pays the interest. Interest amounts can be small amounts, it is the power of compounding that can help build wealth over time. Compounding is when you earn interest on interest, and it allows your money to grow over time.

Entrepreneurship

This is the biggest change happening across the globe. More and more young, creative, ambitious and people are starting their own businesses from school clubs, university dorm rooms and garages. We can observe huge shift happening in the average age of new entrepreneurs. Average age is dropping very fast. To support this point, we can take examples of Microsoft and Facebook. Bill Gates and Mark Zuckerberg were millionaires at 26 and 22 respectively. There are so many examples to prove this phenomenon.

People who have the creativity to develop an idea, the confidence to take the risks, and the tenacity to turn the idea into a successful business are the right candidates for entrepreneurship. They inspire would-be business builders. Many parents hope that one day their own child will enjoy the level of success that is attainable through entrepreneurship - not only the potential financial rewards, but also in terms of personal development and fulfillment.

Kids inherently are creative, ambitious, natural negotiators ("I will finish my homework if I can play cricket ... pleeeaaase"), and excited about learning new things. We all want our children to grow up to be self-sufficient, productive members of society, not just in terms of financial stability but also in terms of personal growth and fulfillment. Nurturing this creativity and energy, and showing kids how to do something with it, can help foster their natural entrepreneurial spirit.

Teach kids about economics

Young children are able to grasp simple economic principles and the older they get, the more they can understand. Very young children can learn by role-playing. Older children are receptive to economic concepts such as supply and demand and the family budget. If our child gets pocket money, this can be a great learning opportunity to examine why and how he or she spends his or her hard-earned cash (wants versus needs, choosing between alternatives, etc.).

Encourage creativity and tenacity

Kids come up with crazy ideas all the time? If so, let us encourage them to expand on their ideas, and then do something about it. When a child excitedly says "I want to build a house for my pet cat!" help her do it. Instead of blocking her thought process with negative remarks, help her finding out a way to make it work. The more a child practices taking an idea and turning it into a reality, the more developed his or her skills will be in creativity, problem solving and persistence.

Act on ideas (before someone else does)

Many people come up with a great ideas, do nothing about it and eventually find that someone else has become quite successful with the same concept. A good idea is not worth much if it is not acted on. Teaching kids to go for it, even with a simple playtime idea, can have lasting rewards. If the child wants to earn money, ask him or her to write down several ideas and then help him or her act on the best one. This way, when a really innovative idea is born, our child will have the skills to take the idea to the next step.

Let kids make mistakes

If we get more protective about exposing our kids to simple problems and fix a problem before a child has a chance to, we rob him or her of the valuable opportunity to learn from his or her mistakes. You can tell that your daughter's idea of building the home for cat is flawed, but, as long as she's not going to get hurt, it is important to let her try her idea. Once she realizes it won't work, you can help guide her toward a better solution.

When evaluating what went wrong, it is important to be honest so kids recognize their mistakes, rather than blaming something else for the failure. This ability to make mistakes and learn from them is critical to the success of an individual.

Teach kids to set goals

Learning how to set a goal and outlining the steps necessary for its achievement is an important skill to have as an entrepreneur. It is simple for kids to wish for things (i.e., "I wish I had a sports bike") but it's a whole different animal to set a specific goal and determine what needs to happen to reach that goal. Here again, setting the goal is usually the easier part; figuring out how to get there is the challenge. Help your child narrow down a clear goal ("I want to earn 12000 rupees so I can buy a sports bike") and then create a budget to help her reach the goal. Having a goal on paper is harder to ignore than just saying "I wish I had a sports bike." The experience can be priceless.

Frauds and precautions

Many kids today are far more computer literate and tech savvy than their parents. Combine that with the growing number of ways to bank, save and invest online, and your child may be entering personal information on one or more Web sites. It is important to maintain online awareness and take steps to protect your child and his or her identity.

Limiting risks

We can't completely eliminate the risk of frauds, we can take certain steps to minimize risk:

Keep paper records, such as birth certificates and ID proofs, other documents in a secure place.

Make sure that all the unnecessary documents and their copies are disposed off.

Be aware of events that make it easier for fraudsters to get your child's information, such as home break-ins, lost purses/wallets/paperwork, security breaches at any place that has your child's information (like a doctor's office or school).

Be aware of your child's online activity. Help him or her set up any accounts (such as for "virtual" piggy banks, or actual bank accounts and make sure he or she is not providing any sensitive information.

Teach your child to use strong email and account passwords (longer passwords with a combination of lower case and upper case letters, and number and symbols, are more difficult to crack.) Instruct your child not to share login and password information with anyone (except you).

Use reputable computer security software and keep it up to date.

Teach your child to avoid clicking on any links embedded in emails or that appear in a pop-up message.

Tell your child that no bank (or credit card company, etc.) will ever ask for personal information via email. As such, instruct your child to never reply to emails, texts or pop-up messages that request this type of information.

Many financial experts and educators believe that the earlier kids begin learning about money, the better their chances for financial stability in the future. You have a great opportunity to help set up your child for a lifetime of financial responsibility by starting the conversation - get your child interested in and excited to talk about money.

We have been discussing about educating children of different age groups in schools or in colleges before they actually start working. There are a number of examples of entrepreneurs who have left the schools to start their businesses and have achieved tremendous success in business.

Some example of entrepreneurs who did not finish school are Steve Jobs - Apple, Bill Gates - Microsoft, Michael Dell - Dell, Henry Ford – Ford Motors, Kemmons Wilson – Holiday Inn Hotels, Jerry Yang – yahoo, Mark Zuckerberg - Facebook, Ted Turner – CNN, J K Rowling – Harry Potter Series Writer, Col Harland Sanders – KFC, David Neeleman – Jet Blue Airlines, John D Rockefeller, Sr. Ray Kroc – Mcdonalds, Ralph Lauren – Polo, Machael Lazaridis – Blackberry (RIM), Tom Anderson – myspace, Walt Disney, Larry Ellison – Oracle, Albert Einstein and Thomas Edison.

CHAPTER 4

WHY ARE WE SO CASUAL ABOUT HEALTH?

We will cover one of the most important aspect of our life, Health. This is the foundation of our very life. We can develop any skillsets or learn any new language anytime provided our health condition is good.

Healthy body and sound mind are the two most important assets we should be protecting and nurturing all our lives. Any lapse in maintaining our healthy body and mind can be extremely dangerous. We will not limit the need of being healthy only for achieving professional success. Professional success is one of the many aspects of living a healthy, happy and prosperous life.

Having worked in Information Technology field for a long time, and being a Production Engineer by qualification, I cannot help but draw an analogy of our Body-Mind with Hardware-Software aspects of Human body and Modern age computing systems.

Human body can be considered as enterprise grade, feature rich, technically advanced, scalable and highly available software installed on a very energy efficient, superior performance oriented, scalable, low maintenance plug and play hardware.

Initially the software was installed only for taking care of day-to-day routine low CPU intensive tasks such as hunting, farming. As the number of tasks to be processed and completed kept on increasing, our motherboards and CPU cores got upgraded continuously. The continuous up gradation of software and hardware was happening in linear proportion till the first industrial revolution changed the way human beings were leading their lives in the late 18th century. The up-gradation process of hardware and software started getting asymmetric during the next 200 odd years.

In the last 200 years, unfortunately due to various social, economic, environmental changes and astounding progress made by Human beings in the field of science and technology, the up gradation and routine maintenance process of the hardware and software has changed drastically.

Regular maintenance schedules of the hardware are not followed properly. Different components of the hardware are getting damaged due to underutilization or overutilization and their performance is degrading year on year. On the other hand, our performance criterion from the software are getting very complex and extremely processor intensive. Regular operating system or security patches are not getting deployed on the software. Software bugs are getting exploited by viruses and external predators. Due to immense increase in the processing required to meet the new performance parameters, hardware has started getting overheated and blown sometimes. Hardware performance is the biggest concern along with patching the software with recent security and operating system updates to improve security and efficiency of the system.

We are reaching a stage wherein, if the software was processing 4 GB data per year two hundred years ago, we are expecting 32GB data to be processed daily using the same software on a less healthy hardware.

In short, we are running most advanced and processor intensive software on an ancient hardware. This is a recipe for disaster. There are instances of software getting crashed due to fatal system error, buffer overflow and lack of database performance fine-tuning or hardware getting overheated due to excessive heat generation and lack of precision cooling, gets blown up resulting into complete system failure and a fire in the data center.

The analogy is so amazingly similar to our mind-body system setup. Obviously, we have designed IT systems after observing our own architecture. We are taking utmost care of preventing fatal system errors, or buffer overflows or DB performance fine-tuning or overheating motherboards and lack of cooling in the data centers to avoid complete system breakdowns to avoid business loss but......

But are we taking care of our own hardware?

Are we taking care of regular maintenance schedules?

Are we taking care of proper precision cooling to avoid overheating?

Are we updating our software with regular security and performance related patches?

Are we making sure that the CPU utilization is optimum by allocating particular process a certain percentage CPU utilization only?

Are we terminating all the unused processes/sessions consuming CPU utilization, to free up costly CPU resources?

Are we waiting for our complete system breakdown?

In case of our complete system breakdown, who will take care of our business of life?

These are the pertinent questions to be asked when we ignore our awareness about health in the most causal manner.

We need to be extremely cautious about the hardware (body) and the software (Mind) we have got by the grace of the god. The system comes with an End-of-Life notification. It depends on us to use it properly for achieving our objectives without damaging it in any way. We should be mindful about the fact that complete product replacement facility is not available till date.

Let us have a look at different health related topics which are directly associated with our continuous growth and prosperity. We will go through topics such as Mental Health, Healthy Relationships, Healthy Lifestyle and Healthy food which is the cornerstone of our success. I hope we can understand the need for health awareness as a critical life skill. This is the focus of this session.

Why are we squandering all the progress made by human beings?

Life used to be very simple million years ago, wake up and leave your shelter for hunting and collecting food. Walk for 5-10 miles a day, take rest in the afternoon in the shadow of a tree, return to the shelter & family before sunset safely. Share the food with all the community. Eat, sing and make merry! Repeat the agenda everyday till you die!!

Compare this to modern life, Wake up, drive up to the market, park near the lift, reach the food court and have your processed food. Repeat the agenda the next day or simply order home-delivery of the food. The same logic can be applied to working in offices or running our businesses. We have lost the touch with physical exercise.

Some of the modern day diseases and health issues which point towards the changing environment and how our bodies are reacting to it are: Heart disease and Diabetes, Osteoporosis, Myopia, back pain etc.

One more ever growing conflict brewing up is mental and emotional one. Due to immense pressure of competition, market conditions, changing social environment, and financial stress, we are suppressing our emotional needs by trying to convince ourselves about futility of pursuing these interests. Mental thought processes are catering to all the materialistic needs and aspirations at the cost of hobbies and other artistic or creative pursuits.

Our personal and social circumstances are also changing very rapidly. We are social creatures. We used to spend our entire lives in tribes living with 3-4 generations together. Sharing each other's knowledge and helping each other solving our problems. That is a very important support system.

In modern societies, we have started getting separated from our families and relatives by living in nuclear families. We are enjoying our new found freedom but we are missing a very robust support system and guidance of our senior family members. These emotional needs are getting stifled creating mental problems like depression and anxiety. The basic human need of sharing our feelings with near and dear ones is difficult to meet due to our focus on maintaining wonderful virtual lives on the social networks while leading miserable personal lives.

Many of our modern day issues can be taken care of by making necessary changes in our lifestyles without losing the benefits of scientific and technological advances. Simple steps like spending more time outdoors playing or working, eating fresh food, getting enough sleep and cultivating friends and groups of likeminded people will help us a lot.

The most important factors affecting our overall health are:

Mental Health issues related to Financial Illiteracy or life skillset Illiteracy.

Unhealthy Relationships and

Unhealthy Food habits

We will cover Mental/Emotional health Illiteracy, Relationship Illiteracy and Food Illiteracy in this chapter. Financial Illiteracy and Life skill Illiteracy is covered in separate chapters of this book.

Acquired modern day ailments

As discussed above, over the period of centuries, we have taken giant strides in the Industrial, scientific and technological development. All these inventions and progress has resulted into more comfortable and luxurious life for us.

With respective technical inventions, we have started underutilizing certain human capacities and functions. To support this point, let us consider invention of modern day automobile or Car. Before cars were designed and manufactured on industrial scale, biggest modes of transport were trains, bicycles or horse carts. Majority of population was moving from one place to another on their feet or horses. Our bodies are well designed for walking. People used to walk a lot almost daily, resulting into compulsory exercise. Once the cars were made available to masses, they got used to travel from one place to another in their own vehicles like cars. It saved a lot of time, but people gradually stopped walking regularly. Some of us made necessary changes in their life styles and accommodated some form of exercise or walking intentionally, rest of us got comfortable in our vehicles and have lost routine exercise habits overnight. The effect of this disruption cannot be observed in a short period of time like 5-10 years. Today we can observe the effects of lack of activity and sufficient exercise around us. We are getting surrounded by lifestyle diseases.

Let us have a look at some of the ailments that we have acquired due to respective modern life style changes..

Cardiovascular Disease – Lack of physical activity, processed and unhealthy food habits, Stress

Diabetes – Lack of physical activity, processed and unhealthy food, Sugar intake

Depression, Anxiety – Lack of physical exercise, lack of social/personal support system, competition, stress and lack of basic life skills

Chronic respiratory diseases – Pollution, Allergies, smoking

The information above is oversimplified but conveys the point mentioned above.

Such a sorry state of health affairs! Reasons?

Let us understand the possible reasons behind such a sorry state of affairs.

Physical activity

Physical activity is the backbone of our good health. Automation and various gadgets have made our life very easy and lazy. We are using a large number of devices to get our personal, official or social tasks or jobs completed. Biggest household culprits behind the laziness are TVs, their remote controls, Computers, mobile phones, tablets, cars, motor bikes.

Modern businesses are leaving no stones unturned to make us lazier by delivering everything from grocery to video games at home. Now we are talking about smart homes and smart offices supported by Artificial Intelligence, wherein depending on our choices and habits all the relevant work in these houses and offices will be taken care of by these autobots.

I understand Homo Erectus is extinct human species. He was a upright man with a strong backbone. Our modern way of life is sedentary in nature. Our work is sedentary. Our transport is sedentary, our recreation is sedentary, our sports are sedentary, and our education is sedentary. We are taking this whole fad of sedentary lifestyle to epic proportions.

I hope, our era in human evolution doesn't end up being labelled as extinct "Homo Sedentarus". We have acquired heart disease, diabetes, back pain, high blood pressure, Osteoporosis and Depression as a result of our love for comfy chair.

Processed, unseasonal & extremely fast food

Our dietary habits are getting transformed across the globe. Rapid globalization, faster transportation facilities, scientific inventions used for preserving and storing food items over a long period of time are resulting into easy availability of variety of food items, fruits, vegetables across the globe.

Nature is the biggest orchestrator. Human bodies got evolved to consume and digest locally available types of food items, fruits, vegetables etc. Naturally available seasonal fruits and vegetables were the right type of food to be consumed by everybody. Limited amount of cooking and seasoning with local ingredients used to cater to the dietary needs of the population. We are not following any of these natural principles of diet and metabolism.

We are ditching our traditional dietary habits and cooking methods while adopting new cooking methods and food items. There is nothing wrong in these cooking methods or food items, we need to understand if these cooking methods and food items are adding nutrients to our diet or they are just plain and simple fast food items. We are getting used to convenience foods to minimize the time required to procure and prepare food. We are not taking a long term view of these eating habits and potential bad effects it can have on our health. These unnatural food habits are resulting into a wide range of health issues including obesity, heart disease, high blood pressure, diabetes and depression.

Cluttered mind and polluted surroundings

Stress is one of the biggest factor behind declining health conditions across the globe. Stress is playing havoc with mental and physical health of an individual. Stress related diseases have grown exponentially and are affecting all the sections of the society and age groups.

Air pollution and water pollution are the biggest contributors behind the decline in the health of society. Air pollution caused by motor vehicles or forest fires or by industrial toxic exhaust are causing chronic respiratory diseases. Water pollution is caused due to contamination and discharge of industrial waste directly into water sources. Water being the primary physical need, effects of water pollution are extremely dangerous.

Diseases caused by stress and pollution are heart related disease, chronic respiratory diseases and cancers.

Mental health

Importance of mental health

Mental health is a state of wellbeing in which everybody can face the normal challenges of life while making most of their own potential, devoting their time and energy in achieving objectives and goals in line with the greater good of the society.

The mental and emotional health basically alters the way we feel about ourselves, the quality of your relationships. It helps us manage our feelings, manage stress in a better way while dealing with normal life events of challenges, failures, losses and disappointment.

We are genetically coded to be social creatures. We are hard wired to work together and live together as a team. Our basic instincts are to help each other, to take care of each other, to appreciate each other and to work together to achieve common goals in life. This basic need of being social, makes us form groups, families, clubs, organizations, unions etc. To be happy and alive, we need that sense of participation, sense of sharing and caring, sense of satisfaction of helping each other, sense of growing together. Though these are basic traits of a human being, unfortunately some of us tend to develop characteristics which are anti-social in nature. That is a different aspect altogether.

In current situation, we can very clearly see a huge crisis developing between our inherent emotional, social needs and the stark contrast of our behavior which is pushing us away from real social life.

All of us go through normal life experiences of success, failure, sorrow, happiness, disappointment, rejection, achievement etc. It is always a never ending mix of different contrasting emotions and feelings. Being mentally healthy doesn't mean that we never go through negative experiences or issues but being able to bounce back from the feelings of dejection, stress and failure.

Mental and emotional resiliency helps us maintain our positive attitude. It helps us wade through negative emotions by focusing on positive aspects of the situation or circumstances.

Believing in the possibility of overcoming stress inducing situations and feelings, goes a long way in actually turning them in our favor.

Why this crisis?

According to global estimates, one in every four persons is affected by one or the other mental health problem at some or the other point in their lives.

We should be afraid of the situation, wherein we are not even acknowledging the presence of the mental health crisis and how unprepared we are to deal with it.

There are various reasons behind the dangerous upswing in the mental health related issues. These reasons can be unrealistic expectations, bad parenting styles, financial problems, failed relationships, workplace pressure, peer pressure, social pressures. Let us have a look at some of the contributors:

Out of breath childhood

Children are the biggest victims of modern day race for the pole position. Parents are putting enormous pressure on the kids to learn and perform anything and everything that they themselves failed to do in their lifetime. Parent want kids to excel in studies, they want kids to learn music, painting, karate, tennis, abacus, badminton, dance and what not.. Formal education starts from the age of two with pre-school. Attending school, extra classes and tuitions is the main objective of childhood.

Children are not allowed to spend time playing or enjoying themselves while growing up. Any free time is a strict affair of watching TV or playing video/mobile games. Children are being protected from playgrounds and outdoor games fearing for injuries and infections.

As if, we are preparing blindfolded slaves to realize their parent's unfulfilled dreams of succeeding in every aspect of their life without any basic life skills.

More and more needs

We are relentlessly pursuing material aspects of life. We are spending most of our energy meeting our materialistic needs and wants. We need a car, a house, latest mobile phone, annual vacations, a bigger car, even bigger house, thinnest and smartest mobile phone and the story goes on.

There are two important ways in which this unending thirst of materialistic possessions is making us mentally sick. First of all, we are ignoring most of our personal, social and mental needs by focusing on achieving our material goals. Second point is about financial pressure that we put ourselves in by spending money beyond our income levels. Financial debt is one of the biggest reasons behind mental problems.

Educational system of denouncement

Our education system is focused on high-performers and achieving a record number of A grades. We are expected to excel in academic syllabus. It is the only parameter of judging quality of the student. Students excelling in studies grade-wise or marks-wise are made superheroes by the schools and parents. Rest of the students are denounced as non-achievers and left to fend for themselves.

Admission to higher education programs depends on the grades or marks obtained in the school examinations. Students who cannot get admission in good schools and colleges are considered less intelligent and are treated differently. Vast majority of students are scarred mentally and emotionally in schools and submit themselves into inferiority complex.

These students end up nursing their mental health issues throughout their lives.

Workplace stress

The work place environment is the biggest contributor of stress and performance related anxiety. Every year the high performers are rewarded with all kinds of awards and incentives. Anyone not meeting the targets set is bound to feel all kinds of negative sentiments leading to mental health problems. If they continuously do not meet targets, they would most likely be asked to leave the company rendering them jobless resulting into even more mental health problems.

Spirituality

With the mind focused on the materialistic possessions and the struggle to survive there is often no time left for any spiritual contemplation. When the stress gets too much to bear and there is no spiritual mindset to help withstand the pressure, mental health problems arise. Spirituality is an essential ingredient for harmonious living in any community. Spirituality is not limited to religion.

Simple lifestyle

Our lifestyles are changing drastically. Commercial world is pushing all kinds of different products and gadgets to us for our instant consumption. Instead of deliberating on whether we needs these devices, we lap up the offers without giving it a thought. Intense peer pressure and our need to conform to society standards, we end up buying or possessing everything that our peers or neighbors or friends buy.

We need to have a very strong mind and strong support from our family to avoid these unhealthy tendencies of spending our energy, time and money on unnecessary devices.

At a personal level

To avoid these modern day traps, we should follow simple basic guidelines:

Live simple. Know your needs versus your wants and reduce meaningless consumption. Take time to enjoy the simple things in life.

Cut the addiction of gadgets and spend more time with family conversations, outdoor activities or pursuing hobbies.

Avoid spending money and time on buying products simply because they are advertised in a nice way.

Set meaningful and realistic goals. Feeling good about the future is important for our happiness. Goals motivate us and challenge us to grow personally and professionally. Setting unrealistic goals leads to stress and mental health problems.

We need to reduce the workload and competition in the schools. Students should be rewarded for their efforts and not just for the results.

Stress and anxiety are parts of our feelings. As we discussed earlier, we are expected to perform well all the time, achieve success and happiness by the standards set by the society. We are facing grave situation of not having mental, emotional and social support systems in place. Due to our increased tendency to keep up to ourselves, we have lost emotional touch with our families, elders, friends and relatives. These are the most dependable support systems we can think of. We are losing our social, moral and professional compass which used to navigate us in difficult times.

Working towards overcoming obstacles to mental health

First step in defeating the mental health issue is to accept that there is an issue which needs immediate attention and resolution before it goes out of our hands. Prescribing anti-depressants and mood altering drugs will suppress the problem for some time. We need to find a solution of eradicating the root cause of the issue.

Anyone can suffer from mental or emotional health problems. Over a lifetime most of us will. Mental health problems being so common today, most of us don't make any effort to improve our situation. We ignore the emotional messages that tell us something is wrong and try braving it out by distracting ourselves with alcohol, drugs, or self-destructive behaviors. We hide our mental issues in the hope that others won't notice them. But our emotional issues always affect those around us, especially when we erupt in rage or despair at the slightest hint of discomfort.

Our reluctance to address mental health needs originates from a variety of reasons:

In some societies, mental and emotional issues are seen as a sign of weakness.

Many of us fail to express our concerns or problems to near and dear ones. We expect these issues to wear out automatically. Egos also play a very important part in not sharing our problems with others.

We focus on taking care of symptoms of the issues instead of root causes. Taking an anti-depressant pill helps us for a while, but the root cause of depression remains unattended.

Maintaining mental and emotional health is not a one-time task. It is a continuous activity. Especially when we are putting immense pressure on brain to perform a lot of heavy duty tasks, it becomes even more important to maintain mental health properly.

How mental & emotional health gets compromised?

Our genetic and biological makeup along with our life experiences shape our mental and emotional health right from the childhood. Typical factors which compromise mental health are:

Poor Upbringing and Relationships: Lack of emotional attachment with people near you while growing up is one of the biggest reasons why we feel lonely, unsafe, confused and reluctant to trust others.

Death of a parent or some tragic incidents early in life also can affect our mental makeup and health.

A very common feeling that comes with negative experiences is belief that we're helpless and have no control over our life

Prolonged illnesses isolate us from ourselves as well as others.

Multiple Medications can have various side effects which can cause mental health issues.

Alcohol and drug abuse can cause serious health problems and or complications in the preexisting illnesses.

Irrespective of our past experiences or circumstances, we can always forget the past and look ahead with positive attitude. Positive attitude supported by intentional efforts in the right direction can help us overcome mental and emotional health issues quickly and effectively.

Maintaining mental & emotional health

Our mental and emotional health influences our daily behavior. It affects how we think, feel, and behave in daily life. It also affects our ability to manage stress, overcome challenges, build relationships, and recover from failures and disappointments.

Our objective can be to take care of a particular mental health issue or simply handling disturbing emotions in a better way, or simply to feel more positive, energetic, and focused, there are various steps we can take to control our mental health. These steps can help boost our mood, build resilience, and increase our overall mental health.

Interacting with people in person

We are social creatures with an innate need for relationships and positive connections with others. We need positive people around us. Face to face interactions are the most effective way to soothe our nervousness and relieve stress. While stressed out, if we can have a word with a person, it helps break the stressful train of thoughts and brings us back on track. It makes us feel more secure just by talking to someone. It is the result of mechanism of sharing built in our systems. The key is to select a person who trusts you and listens to you without interrupting or judging or criticizing.

Asking for help or sharing our concerns is not a sign of weakness. Being open to interactions with the people around us is generally a good idea of building relationships. We can initiate conversations with our neighbors, people in the checkout line or on the bus. It takes nothing more than an eye contact, a smile, a friendly greeting and small talk.

Some simple ways and means of building relationships are:

Call a school friend once every month. Arrange a meeting, if possible. Exercise buddies are good examples of healthy competition and mutual benefits.

Reaching out to new people and making new friends is not an easy task. Be the one to initiate the dialogue. Ask a neighbor to join you for tea.

Prefer real-world interactions compared to online virtual communications.

Joining different social or special interest groups who meet on a regular basis is a good way to start building relations.

Never be afraid to smile and say something pleasant to strangers we cross paths with.

Active lifestyle

Physical activities are an essential part our daily routine. When we improve our physical health, it automatically reflects in our mental and emotional energy. Physical exercise releases powerful chemicals which lift our mood and vitalizes our organs and senses. Regular exercise can have a major impact on our mental and emotional well-being. It relieves stress, improves memory and helps us sleep better.

Understandably enough, not everybody loves exercise. But to achieve good fitness levels, we don't have to be a fitness freak, we don't have to spend countless hours pumping weights or jogging on the treadmills in the gym. Lunchtime walk in the park near office or laps of a shopping mall (of course without shopping), or a dance with our kids, cycling in the woods can be great ways of improving our mental and emotional health. The best part is we don't have to buy fancy gadgets or equipment to start these activities. We can immediately start these exercises.

Small steps can go a long way in improving our health. 30-40 minutes of daily activities like walking, running, swimming, dancing can do wonders to our well-being.

Stress management

Stress is the biggest culprit behind our deteriorating mental, emotional and physical health. Stress affects our life in many ways. There are various ways and means of managing the stress. One extremely logical and easy method of managing the stress instantly is breaking the stress inducing thought train.

This can be achieved instantly by changing our mental and sensory focus from the reason behind the stress onto one of our own senses like sight or sound or taste or smell or touch. Stress balls are the perfect examples of this technique. Other simple things we can do instantly are smelling a coffee and focusing on the actual smell of the coffee, or listening to the song, humming the song ourselves. These activities force us to concentrate on soothing and relaxing things instead of fretting about the stress inducing thoughts.

Most of the times, accepting the unpleasant facts and situations helps us manage our stress in a far better way. Biggest reason behind stress is our unwillingness to accept the things and facts as they are.

Food for thought

We will be surprised to know how our diet affects the functioning of our brains and our psychological makeup. An unhealthy diet can take a toll on our brain and mood, disrupt our sleep, sap our energy and weaken our immunity system.

A wholesome diet, low in sugar and rich in healthy fats can improve our mental capacity and energy. We have different food habits and dietary requirements. Let us have a look at some of the healthy and unhealthy food items: Foods that adversely affect health are alcohol, trans-fats, foods with chemical preservatives or hormones, Sugary snacks, fried food. Foods that boost our health are fishes rich in Omega 3, nuts-walnuts, almonds, cashews, Avocados, flaxseed, bean, leafy greens and fresh fruits.

Sleep

Our hectic schedules are making us cut on our sleeping hours. Getting enough quality sleep is a necessity for our mental and emotional health. Skipping a few hours of sleep can take a toll on our energy levels, mental ability and our ability to handle stress. Continuous sleep deprivation can cause considerable loss of our brain capacity and mental health.

Adults typically need seven to nine hours of quality sleep each night. We need to stop stimulation of our eyes well before going to sleep. TV, Mobile phones, tablets and computers should be avoided at least an hour before bedtime. If anxiety or worrying is disturbing your sleep cycles, we should try and calm our mind down by listening to soothing music or taking a warm bath.

Our body needs time to recover and rejuvenate. Sleeping is the necessary rest for the body. We should stick to regular sleeping schedule.

Find focus

Each one of us works in different ways to achieve our goals and objectives. We should look for engaging work that challenges us to create something or to learn something. These things keep us focused without paying attention to any negative thoughts or circumstances.

Helping others in some or the other way also boosts our self-esteem and confidence. Spending quality time with our family and friends helps us in staying grounded and positive.

Keeping a diary

Keeping a diary is an excellent way of tracking achievement, expressing positive/negative personal feelings and gratitude.

Having a certain target about writing in the diary per day can be beneficial. Such targets can be 3 things to be grateful for or 3 things that could be accomplished today. Or we can have a limit of minimum words per day.

Start your day with your favorite small task

Start your day with a small but your favorite task. It can be having a freshly ground coffee or a stroll in the park or reading a section from your favorite book. It Boosts our morale and lifts our mood.

Plan for a picnic or a vacation

Planning for a picnic or a vacation with family or friends is a very enjoyable process. Having something to look forward to can boost our happiness and morale till the actual picnic or vacation gets over.

Build on your strengths

Do something you're good at. It builds the confidence. We can then tackle tougher tasks

Don't focus on the whole staircase, just take the first step

Decide a goal to be achieved and work relentlessly one step at a time without taking the pressure.

Try new things

Experiment with your favorite recipe or favorite badminton smash. Creativity is essential part of mental health.

Boost brainpower with couple of dark chocolates every now and then

Dark chocolates improve alertness and mental skills. Treat your brain with dark chocolate once in a while.

Share your story

If you have a personal story of achieving an objective in the face of adversity such as illness, share it with everybody. You will feel better and others will be benefitted from your experience.

Sometimes don't add new activities to get more pleasure

Sometimes, it is important to focus on what we have got. These is no point in losing our peace of mind on things we don't have. We must appreciate the things which we already possess.

Remember the good times

When under pressure, revisiting good old memories helps negate the stress and pressure.

Laugh wholeheartedly

Watch a favorite comedy clip or spend some time with funny friend or read a funny book. Spending time with morning laughter clubs is a riot. Laugh wholeheartedly without any inhibitions.

Online blackout

Take a break from social networking sites and online presence. Forget charging your smartphone for a day and get lost in the woods.

Dance around while doing housework

Enjoying whatever we do is the best way of completing the task efficiently within the given timeframe. It improves productivity.

Write it down

If something is making you extremely happy or is bothering you, write it down on the paper. It helps us look at it from a different perspective.

Be with your best friend

Spending your time with pets lowers the stress and makes us feel happy. Best friends also can generate the same feelings.

Be a tourist in your town

It makes us look at our place with a very different point of view. Instead of focusing on issues and problems, we start looking for tourist attractions, favorite food hubs, interesting places to visit, meeting new people.

Practice forgiveness

Forgiveness is very important for mental health. Carrying garbage of ill-will towards people can be very taxing. It saps our energy. Forgiving and forgetting makes a lot of room for happiness in our mind. Don't let our life become a garbage truck.

Try and find out the silver lining

Behind every problem we face, there always is an opportunity waiting for us. We need to focus on the opportunity hidden behind the problem.

Feeling stressed? Smile

Smiling helps lower our heart rate and reduce stress.

Appreciate people

Appreciate people for helping you out. Sending a hand written thank you note goes a long way in cementing the friendship

Do something with friends and family

Arrange small get-togethers for family and friends.

Go for a walk in the nature

Spending time in nature boosts our energy and positivity.

Try something new and make mistakes

Get out of your comfort zone and try something new. Learning a new language or a skill can be a good way to stimulate your brain and creativity.

B. Healthy relationships

Relationships are the mutually beneficial associations we seek for our personal and or professional growth. Relationships can be personal or professional in nature. Following pointers apply to personal as well as professional relationships.

What is a healthy relationship?

Healthy relationship is an attitude we have towards each other. Healthy relationship is having understanding and appreciation of the other person's characters, values and weaknesses. It is a commitment towards helping each other grow together by working on mutual weaknesses and building on individual strengths.

Healthy relationships consists of mutual admiration and love for each other. They are based on serving each other's interests in the friendly atmosphere by communicating very honestly with each other. Healthy relationships are based on common purpose. Common purpose binds the people in relationship together.

Most of us are not perfect in any sense. Healthy relationships are about having patience to see ourselves and the other person work on the weaknesses and grow. It is about loyally standing by each other in happiness and in sorrow, in success and in failure.

Disagreements are a natural part of healthy relationships. Trying to resolve conflicts in a fair and rational manner by way of compromising, if necessary is a hallmark of a healthy relationship. Being supportive by encouraging each other and respecting each other's privacy helps build healthy and long-lasting relationships.

Most importantly, healthy relationships are funny, enjoyable and trustworthy associations to be in. healthy relationships makes us the best person we can be.

What isn't a healthy relationship?

When relationships are based on power struggles and ego issues, they start getting counter-productive. If the objective of being in the relationship is to control others and exploit them using power, then the relationships are doomed to fail acrimoniously.

The methods of dominating others in a relationship ranges from accusations, shouting and yelling, abusive behaviors and possessiveness. Once these mental harassment methods are surpassed, physical abuse or harm starts in the form of pushing, beating up etc. It is always better to notice these common traits of behavior in the very early stages of relationship and to get out of the potentially unpleasant and harmful situation in time.

If we think that our relationship is unhealthy, it's important to think about our safety. Consider these points as you move forward:

We need to understand that a person can change only if he wants to, we cannot force anybody to change their behavior if they fail to accept their mistakes.

Always observe various relationship health indicators. Is the relationship helping us meet our needs? Are we taking better care of ourselves? Are we feeling stressed out in a relationship? If the relationship is putting unnecessary pressure on you, it is better to discuss with partner or with friends who can understand and guide us. We should be strong enough to try all the means necessary to save the relationship but if it is not working out, we should opt out of it.

Always keep our friends, family, and relatives close to ourselves. Maintain good relationships with them. Help them whenever they need us. These are the support systems which will help us in our difficult times.

Creating healthy boundaries proactively

Discussing and agreeing upon some basic boundaries right at the beginning of the relationships saves a lot of heartache and agony. It also sets expectations right. Boundaries are basically a set of ground rules around which our interactions can be based upon. It is a way of guarding our privacy, safety and interests by preventing others from taking us for granted.

Boundaries are not a sign of distrust or secrecy. It is about clarifying about what makes us uncomfortable and what we would like to prevent from happening in the relationship.

Nurturing healthy relationships

Every relationship or association tends to get boring and monotonous over a period of time. We need to nurture relationships by throwing in some pleasant surprises and interesting ways of enjoying each other's company. Simple acts of exercising together, taking a walk together, attending seminars, watching movies, going for a long drive, following nature trails together can boost our relationships.

Healthy lifestyle

Our busy schedules are taking a toll on health of our complete family. Rushing through daily schedules makes it hard to be physically active. It also affects our food habits, resulting into choosing unhealthy snacks and fast food to save time. Spending our spare time in front of TV or computers instead of playing outdoor games and taking a walk in the park are not good choices.

These choices can be dangerous for our health and our children's health. It is important to stop and take stock of the situation so that corrective actions can be taken immediately before the damage caused is irreversible.

Let us have a look at some simple ways of improving lifestyle of kids:

Regular physical activity preferably outdoor ones. It helps kids develop their personality and mental toughness. 60 minutes of physical activity every day, helps strengthen their muscles and bones

Water should be the only medium used for quenching their thirst. Soft drinks, packaged fruit juices and other sweetened drinks should be avoided. Milk is a great source of calcium. Eating natural fruits and vegetables every day helps children boost their vitality and develop strong immunity against multiple diseases.

Avoid spending time watching TV or online surfing or playing computer games. Sedentary lifestyles are making our kids obese and overweight. Plan multiple interesting indoor/ outdoor games or activities for our children.

Healthy snacks helps us meet our daily nutritional needs. Fruits/vegetables, reduced fat dairy products or whole grains based snacks are the healthiest options for us. We must avoid snacks that are high in sugar, salts and saturated fats such as chips, cakes and chocolates.

Simple ways of improving healthy lifestyle

Healthy living is not a one-step solution, it is a continuous long term process which needs commitment and dedication.

There are simple steps we can take right now that will make us healthier.

Check your health status

First step towards improving lifestyle is to understand our current health status. It gives us an idea about where we stand on the health parameters. We can start with regular health checkups, monitoring BMI and waistlines.

Keeping track of our physical activities in a typical week and its intensity, also helps us making necessary adjustments in the daily schedule. Strictly monitoring and controlling food habits goes a long way in keeping health in excellent condition.

Most of the modern day disease are caused by imbalance in the input (i.e. Food Intake) and output (i.e. Proper Utilization of the energy created from food intake). If the energy is not utilized fully and properly, body tends to gain unhealthy weight.

Our body is a very efficient machine. We can keep track of our physical and mental health, by simply observing and monitoring the signals or reactions our body gives to us. Simple indicators to be observed continuously are our moods and energy levels. Are we suffering from frequent mood swings, or loss of sleep or physical symptoms like continuous pain in a part of the body? These pointers indicate towards something going wrong with the body and mind. We can then try and find out the reasons behind the discomfort. Strength of our relationships and social activities also help us a lot in maintaining healthy lifestyle.

Taking corrective measures

Once we understand the areas in which we need the improvement, we can think of multiple ways of controlling these aspects which are causing the discomfort. We should rely on help from the experts in the respective fields to handle the physical and mental discomforts.

Burn the calories

Burning the calories is the easiest solution of most of our issues. What we mean by burning the calories is to exercise and increase physical activities. Physical activities can be rigorous gym training or simple day to day acts of cycling, swimming, hiking, running etc. All of us have our favorite types of physical forms of exercises. We just need to decide which one to work on while enjoying doing it.

Setting personal goals for different activities per week and continuously monitoring it helps a lot. Simple changes in daily routines can make a positive difference. Taking stairs instead of a lift in the building, parking car farthest from the doors of the building, using pedometer to track daily steps taken, walking down short distances instead of using a car. These changes are easy to implement. We can start working on the same immediately.

Watch your food

There has been a lot of discussion happening around diet and controlling food habits. Easiest solution to control and improve our food habits is to make sure that unhealthy food is not available when we are looking for food. We can prepare a list of groceries and food items in such a way that only healthy food items are part of the list and unhealthy ones are completely avoided. Whenever we are looking for something to eat in our house, only options available to us should be healthy ones.

Similarly, while visiting restaurants and food joints, it is better to prepare a list of these places where only healthy food items are available. It can be difficult to find such places but we can keep on searching for such places while avoiding fast food joints.

Literally watching our food while eating it makes a lot of difference. It helps us enjoy the aroma, vibrant colors and texture of the food instead of just gulping it down without chewing it properly. It also means that we should be watching our food and not the TV while eating it.

Biggest building blocks of healthy living

We have discussed various aspects of Mental, emotional, physical health in the topics above. Two of the biggest building blocks of Healthy Lifestyle are Food and Exercise.

The root cause of our nightmarish health conditions is the imbalance between the intake of the calories and the burning of the calories. Our body gets the calories from the food we consume, whereas calories are burnt when our body is used for doing some physical or mental work. It is found that 20% of our total calorie consumption in our body is by brain, remaining 80% of the calories are consumed by remaining organs and systems which make our body tick 24 hours per day, seven days a week. Only solution to this problem which is threatening our society is to control consumption of calories in the right manner and simultaneous increase in burning the calories by exercising and keeping ourselves physically active. Let us focus on these aspects in the following session:

Food

Food is the most essential part of keeping our body going on and on. It is the fuel that is used to crank our systems and processes. The basic role food plays in our lives is as follows:

The Fuel - The most critical function, food plays is to act like a fuel generator. Food consumed gets digested and converted into calories and other substances necessary for functioning of our complex machine - body. Calories are used for performing all the life-critical functions, all our organs, brain, sensory systems, nervous system, blood circulation and pumping, digestion, excretion, cell growth, everything needs calories and other nutrients to work properly. Any variations in the supply of calories to our body results into immediate degradation in performance and causes damage to certain parts, if these variations are not controlled properly.

Food is the main source of nutrients like vitamins, carbohydrates, proteins which are essential for smooth functioning of our body. These components help keeping various systems and processes balanced. Any variations in supply of nutrients, affects functions of the body.

Food also has soothing effects on our mind and body. The aroma, vibrant colors, texture and taste of the food soothes our nerves and makes us feel happy and content.

Choices that we make every day about what we feed our body and mind, makes us who we are mentally and physically. It makes a world of difference in our mental attitudes, energy levels and performance. By opting for foods that improve our strength and reduce risk of illnesses, we are helping our body maintain its longevity without losing its functional capacity.

We should focus on the foods that provide nourishment and avoid fast food which does not provide any nutritional benefits.

Let us have a look at some Good and the bad food options available:

The best options:

Green Vegetables- Leafy and Non-Leafy Green vegetables are a best sources of micronutrients, detoxifying compounds and phytochemicals.

Tomatoes - Tomatoes have strong anti-oxidant and anti-inflammatory properties that help to protect against cancer and cardiovascular disease.

Seeds - Seed provide all the advantages of nuts plus some of the seeds provide Omega 3 fats and anti-cancer agents (Flax seeds)

Nuts - Walnuts, pistachio and almonds are rich in various healthy components, minerals, and other health-promoting nutrients and protects us against heart related ailments

Mushrooms - Mushrooms protect against respiratory infections and various other diseases

Onions & Garlic - Onions, and Garlic supply anti-cancer, anti-inflammatory and antioxidant compounds

Cherries & Pomegranates - Cherries and pomegranates protect against heart disease, cancer. It improves cognitive abilities

Beans – Versatile beans and legumes contact high levels of soluble and insoluble fiber and resistant starch

Berries – Berries support heart health, improve blood glucose levels and reduce inflammation. Berries are happy and rich family of blueberries, raspberries, strawberries and blackberries

The worst options:

Commercially Baked Food Items – Commercially baked food contain refined carbohydrates made from white flour, sugar and oils which are linked to depression and dementia. Avoiding margarines, shortening agents and fast food which may contain trans-fats that accelerate heart diseases is a better option.

Butter - Butter is linked to higher cholesterol, higher rates of heart disease

Pancakes & Donuts – They are high in white flour, sweeteners and oil which are then fried. All of which magnify our risk of heart disease and cancer

Soda – The phosphoric acid in sodas may cause calcium loss, Artificial sweeteners in diet sodas disrupt the body's connection between taste and nourishment, that's why even sugar free sodas are dangerous

Fried Foods – Fired foods like fried chicken, French fries form inflammation promoting compounds as they cook, which can cause genetic mutations and increase the risk of cancer.

Highly Salted Food – Excess sodium is linked to high blood pressure, strokes, heart attacks. Autoimmune disease, kidney damage and stomach ailments.

White Sugar and sweeteners – All caloric sweeteners have effects that promote weight gain, heart disease and diabetes.

Sweetened Dairy Products – Ice cream, low-fat ice cream and frozen yogurt are high in dairy protein and concentrated sweetening agents.

This short list can help us make informed decisions while buying groceries from the market and consume them regularly.

A typical lunch or dinner can be a mix of all the above mentioned good food items which can improve our overall physical, mental and emotional health. We can decide on various options from the food categories as per our likes and dislikes.

A typical wholesome balanced meal should include Vegetables, whole grains, fruits and healthy protein cooked in healthy oils along with water, juice or milk. Variety of vegetables should be the biggest part of the food intake. Healthy proteins can be consumed by adding fish, poultry and beans. Variety of whole grains can be accommodated in the daily food like whole-wheat bread and brown rice. Limited amount of healthy oils like olive oil should be used for cooking or for garnishing food plates. Eating plenty of fruits of all colors is a good source of nutrients. Sufficient amount of water/ milk or juice with little or no sugar is necessary for hydration of the body.

A thumb rule that can be very easily used in deciding healthy groceries every day to choose fresh local produce. More colorful local produce means greater nutrients and nourishment. Nature has been the greatest planner and orchestrator of all.

Nature produces the most suitable vegetables, grains and fruits for the people living in specific area. These food items contain the nutrients and nourishment that exactly matches with the seasonal weather conditions and corresponding dietary needs to protect our body from the environmental variations and climatic changes.

BUY LOCAL, BUY SEASONAL and BUY FRESH.

Exercise

We have discussed about the calorie intake part of the Imbalance problem. Now let us have a look at the other side which is consumption of calories in the right way.

It has been proven time and again that the people who exercise daily, lead a healthier and longer happy life. They have a lower risk of many chronic diseases such as heart disease diabetes. Regular physical activities boost our self-image, improves sleep quality and make us feel energetic throughout the day. It helps keep stress levels under control.

Different research papers and studies indicate approx. 150 to 200 minutes of weekly physical exercise. Easiest way of increasing physical activity daily is to start walking/jogging or cycling or participating in various sports and exercise routines.

Important aspect of physical activity is to raise our heart rate and breathing. The physical activities can be moderate or vigorous. Vigorous activities can be more beneficial compared to moderate ones, but the person who is doing the exercise is the right judge to choose between moderate or vigorous activities. Our physical condition of the body should be taken into account before going for vigorous or moderate intensity exercises.

We are spending on an average seven to eight hours sitting at one place and about six to seven hours sleeping. These proportions of sitting and inactive hours make our life a sedentary life. Modern technology is also playing a very important role of a facilitator of sedentary lifestyle by removing need to move from one place to another to do some work. Machines or gadgets are doing most of the mundane work which we used to do by moving from one place to another. Even our work profiles need lesser and lesser manual work as compared to our previous generations.

Let us take a look at the physical exercise scenario for children and adults.

Children and teens

This is the most critical stage of physical and mental development of a human being. The physical activities for children can be aimed primarily at strengthening bones and muscles along with overall body and mental development.

60 Minutes of any form of physical exercise is necessary for children. It can be moderate activity like cycling or playground activities or vigorous activities like running and badminton. Balance between exercise for muscles such as push-ups and exercise for bones such as jumping, martial arts, football or running is necessary.

Typical activities which can improve overall health of children and teens are walking, playing on the ground like cricket or badminton, playing chess, dancing, swimming, running, football, martial arts, gymnastics and cycling.

Building or developing muscles is an integral part of the healthy growth. Muscles strength is necessary for our daily activities. Activities which can help us develop strong muscles are football, badminton, tennis, push-ups, sit-ups, etc.

Bones are the pillars of our body. They stand by us throughout our lives. Bone strengthening activities for children can be games like jumping and climbing activities, skipping rope, walking, running, dancing, football, basketball, badminton, martial arts, aerobics, weight running and any outdoor sport activity which needs running, jumping etc.

Adults

Adults need to focus on aerobic and strength exercises. At least 30 minutes of aerobic activity per day with strength exercise for two or more days per week covering all the major muscles (legs, hips, back, abdomen, chest, shoulders and arms. Depending on personal requirements, proportion of aerobic and strength exercises can be revised. Important aspect is regularity in the exercise activities.

Other than the physical activities, we should make sure that we are not sitting in one place for more than 30 minutes.

Simple aerobic activities like brisk walking, tennis, badminton, hiking, volleyball, basketball can help us raise our heart rate so that we breathe faster. More intense activities include jogging, swimming, football, tennis, skipping rope, martial arts etc.

Building muscle strength can be achieved by working on typical gym sets in repetitions. Typical ways to strengthen our muscles are lifting weights, working with resistance and exercises that use lifting of our body weight such as push-ups and sit-ups.

CHAPTER 5

DISENCHANTED, DISENGAGED, DEPRIVED & DROPPED OUT?

A systematic approach to batch manufacturing

Historically speaking, we had a robust and well developed education system. In India, we were following a very effective and practical way of education system.

Before the outsiders attacked, plundered and ruled vast part of the country, we had a very effective system of education.

There were two major parts of this system. First part was the "Brahmacharya Ashram" i.e. Student Life stage. Wherein a student used to live with his Guru (Teacher) and acquire knowledge of Science, Philosophy, Scriptures, Logic, Practicing self-discipline, working to earn money so that he can pay his teacher "Dakshina" i.e. an offering which is given out of one's capability and willingness. That means, a student used to learn various life skills from his Guru. He used to earn from offering these life skills as a service to other people. Once these offerings were accepted by the Guru, student can enter into second stage of life, which was about starting and raising a family.

The second major part of life skill education was from parents or senior members of the joint family to their children and junior family members. In those days, in a typical self-sufficient village or city, there used to be professionals who used to supply different types of products and services. These professionals used to acquire technology and knowledge from the senior members of the family and parents. In this way, knowledge and technology of the trade used to pass from one generation to another. These were typical family businesses which used to flourish under one roof under the expert supervision of the senior family member. This was a typical Agricultural Model of Education wherein, parents and senior members of the family or Guru, used to sow the seed of life skill and profession in the mind of a young student and used to let it grow and flourish at its own pace and comfort. Guru or parents used to coach and mentor the process of this process of education.

The basic process of learning was based on observations, vivid imagination, visualization, thinking about multiple possibilities and opportunities behind every thought or action or circumstance. The basic function of the brain was to analyze the situation when our ancient ancestors the hunter gatherers were wandering in the open spaces full of dangers like animals and natural disasters searching for food, and decide from the three available options to them: First was to freeze and do nothing, second option was Flight i.e. to run away from the danger and third option was Fight i.e. fight it out. Face the danger present and survive.

The fundamental working of brain is still based on the same principles. We are no longer facing dangers in the open while searching for food. We are no longer facing life and death situations daily because of animal attacks. We are very safe in our modern working and living environment. But the brain functions in the same manner. For every action or thought, our brain applies the same logic of deciding if the action or thought is a potential danger or not. If it perceives the situation to be dangerous, it makes us select one of the three options of Freeze, Flight or Fight and take necessary actions immediately. Our education must teach us to take a well thought out and informed decision under the circumstances. This decision making obviously needs brain to process more data, analyze more options available and take proper action after thinking about all the possible outcomes and consequences.

This level of sophisticated decision making cannot be achieved without using our creative thinking capacity, critical problem solving skills and innovative ideas. For these advanced skills to kick in action, we'll have to train our minds to defer decisions of Freeze, Flight or Fight till we reach to a well informed decisions. This training of mind is the most important missing part of the education system. We are being made to memorize the answers and regurgitate them in the answer sheets to achieve good marks/grades. This method of education is disturbing and destroying our learning process and capacity.

With the invasions by the outsiders, this self-sufficient system of education was destroyed sometimes by accidents or inevitable societal changes but mostly intentionally. These acts were perpetrated in order to destroy the self-reliance of the common populace and to make them lose their pride in their art/profession making them embrace new lines of work. Very highly technical and accomplished professional knowledge and technologies were thus lost in the transfer from one generation to another due to these gaps and lack of documentation. Once self-reliance was destroyed, self-esteem was a natural victim resulting into accepting superiority of the knowledge and technology of the invaders. In the process, we had lost our education system which was a critical part of our ancient culture and history. Many of the nations in the world were having a very primitive or no education system during this period.

At the same time, western countries were making rapid progress in Industrial manufacturing. In the late 18th century, Britain was leading the Industrial revolution based on advances made in Steam powered engines, Mechanical production equipment. This industrial revolution initiated the automation of jobs on a very large scale. The Industries started looking for employees who could perform the batch production tasks over and over again without asking innovative and curious, creative questions. The objective was to have literate employees who could follow the instructions without getting into reasons behind the instructions. This sudden requirement of labor pushed governments and industry think tanks to create New Education factories which could churn huge number of potential employees. These employees were required to learn a certain skill once in their lifetime and to perform their job for the rest of the life using the same skillset. Minor upgrades and revisions in these skillsets, if necessary were required. But the idea was to learn a skill and keep on using the same skill to fulfil prescribed tasks in the company without any possibility of learning a new skill.

As per the industrial demand and government directives, schools and colleges were established with a certain set syllabi where this new batch manufacturing of skilled labors started on industrial, global scale. With the advent of the First industrial revolution with Britain at the forefront and their rule over vast areas of the world, helped in the quick progression of this Industrial batch manufacturing school education system over all of these places and countries. Almost all the countries under British rule immediately adopted the new system of education.

In those days, almost everybody got the job after getting educated in this system. This setup has worked for almost two centuries.

There are no major changes to this Industrial Grade Batch manufacturing education systems, except revision of the syllabus and new methods of teaching students. The basic objective of the education system still remains the same. It is to manufacture batches of intelligent, professional employees with excellent domain knowledge with very limited or completely stifled Creativity, Innovation skills and independent thought processes.

Even after the 1970-1980 industrial revolution built on Electronics and IT Automated production, the education systems are still running the very efficient batch manufacturing of employees with specific domain knowledge. They are not very active on promoting basic life skills or creativity or innovation.

This education system is like a fast food chain. All the products available on the menu can be served very quickly since all the processes required in manufacturing these fast food items are standardized to avoid any deviation or non-conformity from the set standards. Most of the time, fast food items are readily available and almost every time they do not have any nutrition for our mind and body. On the other hand, very few education systems are like Specialty restaurants or Michelin Star restaurants, wherein Creativity and Innovation are the most awarded features.

Unfortunately, this education system based on standardized assembly lines principle, measures the performance of all the students in the system against a fixed set of standardized question sets. Any deviations from the standard answers are not given any marks and hence the students who memorize and regurgitate the answers to these questions pass with flying colors. On the other hand, a student with his own view on the subject comes with an answer which does not conform with the set answers, hence this creative and curious student is not given any marks and fails the exam. Failure in this exam amounts to no chances of getting a job on the automatic assembly line.

How do we learn?

Origin of schools must be very interesting. When books were very rare, mostly handwritten in limited number of copies, sharing the knowledge and information from these books to a lot of people was very difficult. The knowledgeable person who could read the book used to take a center stage, people used to gather around him to listen to his reading and interpretations. As the time passed, with invention of printing and development in the transportation facilities around the globe, availability of the books and other knowledge sources were readily available for all. Very limited people were literate enough to read or write. Hence the lecturing and schooling system of education continued

With the first industrial evolution, need for a large number of literate skilled workers suddenly increased exponentially. The political and thought leaders of the day, extended the traditional schooling system of gathering batches of students around a teacher extended on a large industrial scale. Schools were promoted and literacy was the buzzword of the day. Literacy i.e. reading and writing was the skillset which used to guarantee job for a lifetime.

This schooling system was based on gathering batches of students in neat lines in the classroom depending on the age groups and different domains which were in demand in those days. The classrooms were designed for different age groups depending on the skill sets requirements of the industries. The objective always was to prepare a steady assembly line of skilled workers to do the job without asking any questions or raising any doubts.

Hence the basic human traits of creativity, innovation, arts, music, Dance, Painting were not given equal importance. The skill sets related to Arts, hobbies, life skills like communication, critical thinking, and curiosity were actually out of syllabus. Students were expected to learn these skills by themselves, no systematic approach or systems were put in the place because these skillsets were not needed for the rulers and the decision makers of the day.

With developments in the fields of science and technology, the nature of school complexes and classrooms changed. These changes were limited to teaching methods and devices used in the classrooms, the way subjects were taught in the school, the way students were made to sit in the school and follow strict discipline. Most of the curious and inquisitive questions were left unanswered. Teachers were also victims of this systematic approach of selective education. They were made to follow the syllabus defined by the authorities, any deviation or addition of new subject or topic of his or her interest or of students' interest were not allowed. Teachers and students were made to enlist themselves for extra tuitions for these extra-curricular activities and subjects.

This education system is based on the simple system of "What Teachers Wants To Teach Us". It is never about "What We Want To Learn". This forced education is preventing us from learning things which we really like. Fortunately or unfortunately every human being is different from each other. Their emotional, intellectual, social circumstances and needs are very different from each other. Their aspirations, dreams, ambitions and the resources available with them to work towards achieving their cherished goals also vary to a very large extent. The current education system is standardized assembly line designed to manufacture same type of product on a very large scale. There is no scope for customized and need based education on a personal level. Neither do we have the infrastructure necessary to provide these need based learning nor do we have qualified trainers who can train these individuals on a very large national or global scale.

Students were allowed to use devices of learning like slates, paper sheets, paper notebooks, computers and tablets. The syllabus designed and controlled by society leaders always suited the ever growing demand of the selectively educated labor in the industries.

We have been following the same system of Industrial grade batch manufacturing education system even today.

We are continuously running behind achieving the success parameters set by the society in terms of money and Status symbols. Most of our energy, resources and time is getting utilized in achieving these material goals. In the race to amass more money and related material pleasures, we are completely neglecting the basic principles of our human characteristics such as social interactions, enjoyment and necessary rest for the body. Sleep deprivation is considered a symbol of ambition, getting some rest is considered laziness and getting too busy is considered symbol of importance. We are a lucky generation to have huge knowledge and technical advances making our lives comfortable and luxurious. Never in the history of mankind before, were these resources of knowledge and luxuries of life available. We never had such a technical advancements making our lives comfortable and easy. On the other hand, even after having all these resources handy, never in the history of mankind, were people so stressed, unhealthy and unhappy.

Globalization exposing our weaknesses

Till very recently, our education and employability skills were tested in local industries and job markets. With Information Technology and Globalization, we were forced to compete with the best in the world at the highest levels.

Our educational apparatus was making us ready for the immediate market needs, even then the gap between the skill-sets demanded by the industry and corresponding training in the schools and colleges is widening day by day.

We are being trained for skill sets which are no longer sufficient to take care of our entire careers. People used to cling to a single job for their entire working lives. In the Changed market dynamics and opportunities created by globalization, now most of us are changing at-least 8-10 jobs or work profiles throughout our careers. These different jobs and work profiles are never based on a single skill set. Each job profile needs some or the other skill set to be learnt or improved upon.

We have covered different skill sets requirements of the global workplace in the Soft skills literacy section. These modern age opportunities are going to pit us against the best candidates from different countries with different backgrounds and cultures. It is extremely critical to understand how rapidly our surroundings are changing and what needs to be done to survive and thrive in these circumstances.

Only technical domain knowledge and expertise is not going to be sufficient. Technical domain knowledge, well developed life skills and awareness of making right decisions about utilizing this domain knowledge-life skills for the right reasons at the right time are going to be critical to the growth and success.

The fourth industrial revolution: biggest opportunity or threat?

World Economic Forum has been putting great emphasis on the already In Progress 'Fourth Industrial Revolution', its effects on all of us and how do we prepare ourselves for this fantastic opportunity.

The first industrial revolution was about Steam power and industrial manufacturing. The second industrial revolution was based on the invention of electricity and its use for mechanizing and automating various industries. The third Industrial revolution utilized Internet, Telecommunication and Digital economies and Digital lives. The fourth industrial revolution is expected to bridge the gap between human beings and machines by making machines artificially intelligent and blended with human existence to such as extent that most of the routine or mundane jobs done manually will be handed over to these robots and autonomous systems. These autonomous systems will take real time decisions about our lives based on Artificial Intelligence and technologies like Internet of Things and Big Data analytics. These machines will take care of our smart cities, smart homes and smart cars.

The fourth industrial revolution will be amalgamation of Automation of processes and systems, intelligent machines & robots, nanotechnology and Biotechnology with study of genomics which will change the way we do the things and get the things done from others or systems. Substantial amount of jobs based on basic skill sets will get wiped out overnight. Autonomous systems, computers and machines will replace employees across the industries.

There are very visible skill set gaps in the job market. A large section of society is still struggling to get access to basic education. These sections of the society are deprived from the basic access to literacy. The second section of the society is literate in terms of reading and writing. The third section has got good education from schools, universities in basic faculties of arts, science and commerce. The fourth section is fortunate enough to get access to advanced professional education like engineering or medicine or law or management.

That means there is a large section of the society who is deprived of the education and basic life skills. The other section who has got access to basic education cannot continue with it due to various financial and personal reasons. They simply dropout from the education process. A large majority of people complete their formal education while being completely disengaged from the process of learning. They focus only on passing the examinations and get the degrees or certificates due to family or societal pressures, while their interests lies in different skill sets and professions which are not covered in the regular school/college syllabus.

In totality, a large section of society is disenchanted with the education process at various levels.

The immediate effects of this disenchantment can be observed across all the industries and job markets. Unskilled personnel are not getting any jobs, People with specific skill sets are stuck in regular jobs wherein they cannot practice skills of their choice. The third set is of the people who have learnt one skill and are not ready to upgrade their skill sets. They want to survive their entire working life on a single skillset. Fourth group wants to learn new skills and upgrade their existing skills but facilities and infrastructure is not available. While on the other hand, industries are demanding continuous upgradation of existing skillsets and acquiring new skills. This tug-of-war is creating huge pressure and stress on the Employee-employer relationship across all the sections of the society and the workforce.

Fourth industrial revolution is posing serious threat to all the sections of the workforce. People with different skill proficiencies will have to upgrade and acquire new skills in a very limited timeframe. All the three industrial revolutions have given us sufficient time to prepare ourselves for the changes and adapt to the demands of the market. But this time, with the Fourth Industrial Revolution, we will not have the luxury of time. We'll have to anticipate changes and proactively upgrade or acquire our skill sets and be ready.

If we can take preemptive actions to be ready for the challenge, we are in for a pleasant surprise. If we are uncomfortable with the changes and fail to get ready for the disruption, we are in for a difficult, inconvenient and regrettable but completely avoidable situation.

Problem statement

Learning process: yesterday & today

Our learning process has been designed to reflect availability of the information/knowledge, expected utilization of acquired knowledge and method of knowledge sharing on a larger scale.

Our learning process was designed to take care of Information scarcity due to limited number of handwritten or printed books. Our intelligence was tested by our capacity to recall. The person who could know maximum things was considered intelligent. Things have changed vastly in the last 100 odd years, especially after Internet revolution. Today our learning processes need to reflect changed environment and conditions. We are facing Information Overload/deluge. Our intelligence is tested by our capacity to identify relevant knowledge source from staggering number of good, bad and the worst sources available all around us, Next step is to access the most suitable data for our use and the last point is to understand how to utilize the same for our advantage. Learning processes were standardized for public consumption. Nowadays these processes needs to be customized depending on individual preferences and needs.

Services based economy

We are moving towards a service based economy. Wherein most of the jobs will be customer facing, which means almost all of us will be interacting with our existing and potential clients on a regular basis. Work profiles in services based economy will demand strong communication and collaboration skills along with domain knowledge and interpersonal relationship skills.

Global skill migration crisis

Global political and social dynamics keep on changing very frequently. Some regions are stable where as some of the other regions are in a major turmoil. Most of these volatile situations are beyond the control of majority of the workforce but they end up bearing the brunt of the situation. In such a circumstances, people lose their jobs and livelihood overnight. Most urgent need for them is to earn livelihood by doing whatever job they can get hold of. Their skill sets does not necessarily match with the requirement of these jobs but they do not have any choice. Acquiring new skills in the shortest possible time becomes the need of the hour.

Even under normal circumstances, due to various disruptive changes in the technologies and product/services consumption patterns, a lot of people lose their jobs instantly. The skill sets involved in performing such jobs are valuable but due to sudden lack of demand from the market forces these individuals to acquire new skillsets instantly or within shortest period of time.

Anticipating these changes is not an easy task, but keeping our skill sets updated and always looking for acquiring different skill sets according to our likes and interests is a good way of avoiding such unfortunate circumstances.

Global warming of brains

We have discussed how our ancient hardware of brain is coping with ever increasing burden of modern day performance criteria. Some of the aspects affecting our capacity to think, analyze and draw well thought out conclusions are our learning methods, information processing overload and extremely poor diet.

Our brains were hardwired to analyze situation and to decide on whether to Freeze or Flight or Fight in case of sensing a danger. Our brain functions the best when subjected to open, creative and innovative ideas and situations. Brain functioning gets hampered under closed, standardized routines. It continuously needs stimulation to maintain its health. In some cases, inactivity of the brain even results into diseases related to brain and its functioning.

Information processing requirements also have changed enormously. There is an extremely heavy increase in load considering the fact that no noticeable improvements have taken place with respect to structure and functioning of our brains.

The very important aspect directly affecting our brain function is lack of nutritious diet. Our fast food and processed food diets matched with irregular food eating habits are starving our body and brain of the necessary nourishment and vitality.

Our brain functions and performance levels are degrading very drastically.

These issues related to brain are not isolated incidents but a global epidemic. Increasing stress levels, unhealthy lifestyles, erratic food habits and lack of rest or relaxation due to continuous exposure to innumerable stimulations are resulting into mental health epidemic. This mental health epidemic is threatening us and our continuous growth as human beings. The effects and repercussions of this man made epidemic can be compared to another man made life threatening crisis of Global Warming.

Side effects of technology

Technology can be a double edged sword. It can be a bane or a boon depending on how we utilize and control it. We have harnessed benefits of technological advancement over the centuries. At the same time, we are losing on some of the basic life skills. Unfortunately most of these skills which are directly getting affected are soft skills. Let us have a look.

Handwriting –

It has been a very important basic life skill which has been an essential part of our evolution. Most of the ancient literature, knowledgebase, books were handwritten. Handwriting is considered a mirror of one's personality. Printing is a very recent technical breakthrough compared to handwriting tradition. Nowadays, keyboards of computers or electronic gadgets are taking care of documenting our thoughts instead of writing them down manually. In some cases, even verbal notes can be translated into written text automatically using a software or an application.

There will be occasions where, handwriting will be preferred over printed material. Handwritten notes can be an important personal touch in building long lasting relationships. Most importantly, handwriting will help us jot down our notes when fancy gadgets and applications are not available with us.

Eye contact

Our interactions with people have increased exponentially in recent times. Especially with Social networking sites, these interactions are virtual in nature. While interacting with the people on the internet, most of the time we are not facing each other. Non-verbal communication is a very critical aspect of our communication process. Most of the non-verbal aspect of communication is missing in virtual interactions.

The other aspect of internet communication is the disturbance it is causing in our interpersonal communication. Most of us are so engrossed in checking our mobile phones that we tend to ignore real persons sitting next to us. Even while meeting each other, instead of focusing on face to face conversation with full eye contact, we keep on checking our mobiles and gadgets which results into complete degradation of our interpersonal communication experience.

Making eye contact with the person we are interacting with reflects our self-confidence, high self-esteem. Online social interactions are harming our self-confidence and playing with our self-esteem levels which is directly affecting our ability to have meaningful conversations with real person with good eye contact.

Chitchat

We have tendency to relate and connect to people on daily basis. One of the easiest way of initiating discussions and relationships with strangers is to start with a little chitchat. Discussing topics which are generally unimportant but are of interest to both the parties. It opens up channels of more meaningful dialogues. In our personal and professional lives, meeting new people and networking is very important. A little chitchat gives us a lot of information about character of the person which helps us screen good and bad people to associate with.

Our virtual social interactions on the internet have distracted and disconnected us from real life world. We are expecting a friend request from somebody before we accept his request and start interactions with him or her. In real life, friend requests are made by initiating a little dialogue which is a basic life skill.

Basic arithmetic skills

With penetration of gadgets in our everyday life, we have become totally dependent on these gadgets to help us with basic tasks such as remembering phone numbers, doing basic calculations of addition, subtraction, division and multiplication. We are taking help of electronic devices to help us remember things and do basic arithmetic. Mobile devices are making our life extremely dependent on them right from remembering birthdays or meetings. We are reaching a stage wherein if due to some reasons mobile device is not functioning for some time, we are getting extremely annoyed and helpless. It is affecting our ability to manage basic life information gathering and processing.

We are depriving our brains of basic stimulation which is needed for its healthy functioning. We need to limit use of external devices to keep ourselves in good mental shape to collect, store, analyze and process life related information and data.

Common courtesy and social etiquettes

We are so immersed in our virtual online lives that we are failing to understand our social surroundings which is full of real people. We are getting disconnected from real life to the extent that the basic etiquettes that we follow while interacting with other people or while being in a public place are getting forgotten. We are so focused on ourselves, we are failing to observe a senior citizen standing next to our seat in the bus and offer our seat to him or her. The basic human traits of situational awareness are getting hampered due to our reliance on inputs from our gadgets.

Redundant RAM (Random Access Memory)

We are using new age gadgets to store all our information and are accessing it anytime with a single click of a button. If the information is not available on the gadget, we are immediately searching for the same using Internet. We are not in a position to remember even 5 contact numbers of our closest friends and family members.

These gadgets help us take care of our day to day basic information needs for sure. But we cannot completely rely on these equipment, which are subject to failure. We should be able to lead normal lives in the absence of these devices and gadgets.

These devices are certainly improving our efficiency and productivity resulting into a lot of time saving. Issue is when we start twiddling with our mobile devices or other gadgets aimlessly. Spending our time and energy on these gadgets to keep ourselves engaged or to keep ourselves distracted from the real world is a serious issue.

Loosing on simple pleasures of life

Invasion of our lives with modern technology and superefficient gadgets has helped us achieve some spectacular goals in our daily lives. On the other hand, we are losing on some very basic pleasures of life. We have stopped appreciating simplest and the most obvious gifts from life.

We are using these tools and devices to keep us distracted and disengaged from the realities of our life. We are using these tools to run away from the reality of life. Spending some time with ourselves is critical because it forces us to clear our minds and listen to our thoughts and helps address some issues without any distractions. We are complicating simple things.

Enjoying one thing at a time with complete focus has become an ancient way of living. We are cramming our lives with many things trying to achieve everything at the same time. We are not hardwired to multitasking. We cannot move from one task to another without losing our concentration or focus. Hence doing one thing at a time with complete focus will certainly help us achieve better results while enjoying the task.

Internet fuelled social networks are designed to share our happiness and sorrow with our friends and internet buddies. Unfortunately, these social networks have started creating negativity, hatred and jealousy in some form or the other.

First of all, online social profiles and images are carefully and tactfully presented to showcase our beautiful and happy life. Very few social netizens are showcasing their real persona and life on the social networks. We have started getting jealous and hateful after watching fabulous lives of our friends and buddies on the social networks. We are feeling dejected, stressful and unhappy after surfing the social networking sites. The basic purpose of these tools is getting defeated.

It is therefore, very important for us to limit our usage and dependency on electronic gadgets and social networking sites or Internet images. It is better to focus on our personal lives and real people around us. These modern devices and social persona are only for limited consumption, any kind of overdose will certainly affect our mental, emotional and physical health.

Social marketing and influencing public opinions

Companies with huge interest in ever increasing technology and Internet users are using these platforms to advertise and market their products and services to millions and millions of people. Similarly, these platforms of global public interactions are used by vested interests to influence and subvert popular public opinions by bombarding them with twisted facts and figures.

Internet and its applications are addictive

Internet and its practical applications in day to day life are so ubiquitous, we cannot imagine our lives without these tools. Emails, Social media, discussion forums, internet websites for planning and executing our tasks like booking tickets or vacations or paying fees are so commonplace, we are almost entirely dependent on these facilities. This dependence has reached a level of addiction. We cannot survive a day without checking our emails or social network updates.

Some of us have started getting withdrawal symptom when internet connection is down due to some reason. Internet addiction is becoming a mental health disorder.

False self image, false sense of social acceptance

Constant exposure to internet and social networks have made us aware of importance of building a Virtual Image. This virtual image is built by presenting ourselves in a way that is acceptable to our cyber friends. Constant urge to keep up with the cyber buddies and their cyber lifestyles is putting enormous pressure on us. We are more interested in sharing updates about the fun we are having with our buddies rather than actually having the fun ourselves.

At the same time, we are exposed to deluge of information from all the sides in real and virtual life. Most of the time, the information available to us is not relevant to us but we still have to process it and decide whether we can use it for our benefit or not. This process of decision making about information utilization itself is a huge task. It is putting unnatural stress on our brain and body. Our vital resources like intelligence and time are getting wasted in these activities. While doing so, we have started ignoring real people around us by not caring about them including our own self.

In real life, we can observe, screen and decide whom to be friendly with. We can use our senses and power of observing verbal, Non-verbal cues from the person, whereas in cyber society, the parameters on which we can judge the person are very limited and easy to manipulate. We are sharing our personal experiences and information with strangers based on their images and status updates posted on the internet. As per studies conducted, we can manage meaningful relationships or acquaintances with a very limited persons at a time. Studies suggest that on an average, normal human being can manage around 150 meaningful relationships at a time. Social networks are exposing us to thousands of people on regular basis. The relationships are increasing in numbers and degrading in quality. It is better to have quality associations with a limited number of buddies in real or virtual world rather than having thousands of acquaintances with limited value addition.

People are still analog in this digital world

With all the advancements in the technology, at the end of the day everything revolves around managing, interacting and communicating with real people. All the gadgets, internet applications, social networks, automatic machines have people at their backend, managing, controlling, monitoring them at every step. We cannot trade our life skills with internet skillsets.

We cannot trade off personal, social etiquettes with netiquettes. But we must complement our personal, social life skills with modern technology skill sets and etiquettes.

In the end, it is the lifetime memories, and real life experiences which will stay with us not the social network profile metadata.

Survival without technology

Modern technology is so ingrained in our daily lives, we cannot imagine surviving without the presence of modern gadgets and equipment. We are building a make believe world wherein we can do everything through bits and pieces of technology and access to the internet. Nothing can be farther from the truth. Modern technology is a supplementary tool in our progress and growth. Technology cannot replace human beings, at least in the near foreseeable future.

Digital fast is an interesting idea. Keeping ourselves detached from all types of modern gadgets and technologies is a rejuvenating experience. It is a nice detox. Deactivating social networking site profiles, locking mobile phone and tablet in a house drawer, forgetting to charge laptop and getting lost in the beautiful nature can do wonders with our energy levels and mental health.

We have survived for a long time with or without technology. I am sure we can survive at least one or two days every month with ourselves without any distraction from technology.

These things can only be achieved if we can lead by example. Putting down devices when it's dinnertime, or while watching sports, or while having a conversation is necessary. It makes us focus on the activity without any distractions. We can enjoy our food, or a sports match or a conversation by fully engaging ourselves. Children will model their behavior based on our behaviors.

How globalization is changing the world

We are at a unique juncture of the Transformation, when all of our accumulated knowledge and skillsets will be tried and tested against the ever-changing skillset demand. We'll be forced to acquire new skillsets in shortest possible time to match the demand.

This demand for new skill sets is accompanied by global competition for these jobs and work profiles. People across the globe will be competing for these skillsets and jobs. We have already seen how computer programming, telemarketing, computer systems analysis, accounting and billing functions are getting outsourced to the most cost effective English speaking skilled people.

The next stage will be to automate and outsource these jobs involving repetitive tasks to robots or autonomous systems. This step will result into loss of employment across the layers of the workforce. Unskilled, Semi-skilled and skilled personnel will have to look for other job opportunities by acquiring new skillsets. The training systems of domain knowledge will not be sufficient. Life skillsets such as creativity, innovation and adaptability will be the foundations on which new skillsets will be built upon.

Going by market reports, IEEE says by 2040, 3 out of 4 vehicles are going to be autonomous. Last trillion dollar industry was created by computer code, next trillion dollar industry may be created by genetics code. Unemployment of the technology based workforce is expected when the android starts doing its job using artificial Intelligence and Internet of Things.

Land was the raw material of the Agricultural age. Iron was the raw material of the Industrial age, data is the raw material of the Information age, Concepts & Ideas will be the raw material of the age we are ushering in.

Let us not rely on the system to bail us out. Prince in the shining armor is not coming to save us, we must help ourselves. Internet has become a central nervous system and shared brain of the humanity. Let us migrate ourselves from Social networks, online gaming, chatting and surfing to learning mode. Let us use this collective intelligence and get ready for the new age.

Let us be ready…

Possible solutions

Surviving the transition

We have seen how rapidly things around us are changing. We are going through a period of cultural, social and political upheavals across the globe. All the established myths and hierarchies are getting destroyed, new political leaderships is taking control of the world. New leaders are talking about radical changes in the way we are conducting business around the globe.

The job market is directly related to each other globally. No nation or society can remain untouched or isolated from the effects of global disruptions of any nature. Internet and development of fast transport facilities have brought us together like never before. Skilled workforce is ready to move and relocate to any part of the world, which can offer better job opportunities and better lifestyle. The influx of skilled people from outside are creating enormous pressure on local populace. Unskilled or semiskilled local people are the worst affected because of this influx. The outsiders are ready to take up any job whereas these unskilled native people do not have the skills to compete with outsiders. Social and political tensions have started affecting everybody.

These situations are going to get worse as the time goes by. Fourth industrial revolution will make a lot of jobs redundant. We are not sure how the governments and industries are going to take care of mass skill migration and loss of jobs on a very large scale. Skilled and proactive people will get ready for the change but poor and uneducated section of the society which is large in number will be left to fend for themselves. This is a recipe of political and social unrest and disaster.

Better approach will be to educate people from all the sections of the society about the impending calamity and make them ready for the new era of progress and growth. Only inclusive growth of 6 billion people can help us grow and prosper. Growth of certain pockets without taking everybody along will create huge imbalance in the society. Fruits of the technological revolutions will be meaningless if they are not shared across the sections of the society.

We have covered basic life skills like Health literacy, Financial Literacy and Soft skills literacy in the previous sections. Let us have a look at some additional pointers which can help us build strong foundation of life skills which can be later used for building solid domain expertize and specific skillsets.

Building on our inherent strengths

We are genetically hardwired to observe and select best choice among the available options at our free will. We have innate urge to connect with other human beings, help each other, share and care. These are genetic traits developed over thousands of years of evolution. Our biggest strength has been creativity. We are the most creative and innovative creatures, which has helped us survive and prosper over thousands of years by adapting to different circumstances and situations.

Our body and brain tends to function at its best when it is allowed to function in open environment with minimum restrictions, wherein brain and our senses can observe and look out for dangers, analyze and process information about our continuously evolving surroundings, reach to conclusions about the threat perception from other animals and things and take most suitable action out of three options of "FREEZE or FLIGHT or FIGHT".

Even in modern circumstances our brain follows the same procedures of observations, conclusions and actions. Our surroundings have changed drastically. We are no longer living in caves, hunting in open spaces for daily food, returning to our homes with food and enjoying it with other family members. The main objective of life for human beings was reproduction. Every other actions was aimed at achieving the main objective.

In current scenario, we are living in developed societies with all the luxuries and conveniences available to us. We are no longer facing life threatening situations daily. We are working in protected environments like offices, we are travelling in safe vehicles. Our brains are continuously looking for threats and possible exit options to keep us protected. Under current circumstances, we are expecting brains to leave this function aside and focus on learning new things, processing huge piles of data and deduce possible solutions wherein we can get benefitted in terms of money or satisfaction or happiness. We are expecting our brains not to be in continuous "Alert mode" to initiate flight or fight mode. We want our brains to take a deep breath before going into observation and analysis mode. We want our brains to take another deep breath before assessing the threat perception by considering various reasons behind the situation and various permutations combinations of our responses and its consequences. We want our brains to not run away from the threat or fight with the threat cause. We want our brains to take a rational view of facing the threat without running away or fighting with the cause behind the threat perception. We want our brains to evaluate all possibilities of solving or neutralizing threat perception.

All these steps we want our brains to follow are not natural to normal working of our brain. It is trying its level best to adapt and make necessary changes. Brains are under tremendous pressure to reform themselves within a very short period of time. They have been hardwired for Freeze, Flight or Fight for thousands of years. We are trying to rewire our brains in a very short period of time like 400 to 500 years.

To help our brain develop new ways of working in the shortest possible time, we'll have to train our mind and brain to function in a different way. Our ancestors were extremely scientific and intelligent people. They were aware of the continuous buffer overflow and CPU overload issues. They had discovered very effective ways of keeping our brains in the most effective state and to improve health.

Meditation is one of the most efficient method of improving our control and functioning of mind and brain.

Meditation: our brain & mind trainer

Meditation is not a technique but a way of life. Meditation means 'shutting down the thought process'. It is a state of the mind which is free of scattered thoughts and various patterns. Meditation means awareness. Whatever you do with awareness is meditation. "Watching our breath" is meditation; listening to the birds is meditation. As long as these activities are free from any other distraction to the mind, it is effective meditation.

Meditation can be about focusing on one specific thing, it could be our breathing or particular object or organ in our body. The objective is to focus on one point and trying to bring our attention back to that point when it wanders away again and again. The other method can be paying attention to all the things happening around us, we simply notice everything without reacting.

It has been observed in modern fMRI scans that while meditating our brains stop processing information as actively as it normally does. It has been observed that there are specific changes that happen to parts of our brain while meditating. The frontal lobe, which is responsible for reasoning, planning, emotions and self-conscious awareness tends to go offline while meditating. Parietal lobe is responsible for processing sensory information about the surrounding. During meditation, activity in the parietal lobe slows down. Thalamus which focuses on deciding whether to supply some sensory data to brain or stop it from reaching the brain, reduces the flow of incoming information substantially. Reticular formation reduces the incoming stimuli which makes brain stop from being on alert all the time.

Basically what Meditation is doing is trying to relax brain and mind by reducing its functions to a bare minimum. Most of the mental health issues and stress related ailments, performance issues are product of the overutilization of the brain and mind. Brain being the most critical part of the body needs relaxation and rest from time to time. Meditation helps brain relax and rejuvenate.

Meditation helps improve various aspects of our sensory and cognitive skills. Meditation being a practice of focusing our attention and being aware of when it drifts, improves our focus when we're not meditating as well.

Mediation helps reduce anxiety to a great extent. Typically our bodily sensation and fear centers of the brain are connected by neural pathways which carry these sensations to the Me center (Medial Prefrontal Cortex) which processes this information and makes us feel scary or upsetting or unhappy. When we meditate, we intentionally weaken the connection between bodily sensation and fear centers with Me center. This means that we don't react as strongly to sensations as we normally would have. At the same time during meditation, connection between assessment centers and our bodily sensations & fear centers gets strengthened. When we experience scary or upsetting sensations, it helps us rationally evaluate the situation.

Meditation improves our creative ability, empathy towards others, memory and reduces stress and decline of our cognitive functioning. It leads to more positive emotions, longer lasting emotional stability and focus in our daily lives.

Meditation helps us towards Inner Peace and Outer Dynamism i.e. Peace of Mind and Improved performance levels.

Our learning abilities can also be associated with our capacity to focus on intended things by avoiding distractions. Our brains work in alternating focused mode and diffused mode. Learning different things when our brain is in focused mode gives us better results. Whereas any learning efforts taken when brain is in diffused mode, results into substandard learning.

Our brains function really well when we are in creative or innovative mode of mind. This strength can be used in our learning process. Instead of reading page after page continuously, we should read a page, look away from the page and try to visualize what we have gone through. It makes us memorize concepts, ideas in a better way. Storytelling way of learning is also a very effective way of education. The lesson or concept which needs to be taught can be put in an interesting story format will all the twists and turns. It helps us visualize complete story which improves our understanding of the concept.

Building a solid foundation

Let us go through some of the important points which can help us build a strong approach towards building a solid foundation of learning advanced skillsets. Mere hard work without proper planning and clarity of thought will not yield excellent results. We need to make some changes in which we look at certain aspects of the learning process.

Gaining career capital

While in school or in college or in professional life, our focus needs to change from memorizing subjects or lessons just for the sake of passing examinations or achieving grades. We need to learn these lessons to understand what these concepts, ideas mean and how they can be utilized or worked upon in real life scenario.

Our objective towards learning and educations can be completely altered, if we can observe and analyze how certain concepts or lessons or skills will help us grow in our careers. How these lessons can be used in achieving better results in our personal and professional lives. We can pay comparatively less attention to the pointers which fail to qualify this category and focus more on aspects or lessons which can be used extensively in the long term. We need to help children understand this process and help them make these important distinctions. This process cannot be a one- time activity, it needs to be a continuously evolving process of screening.

Develop skills, learn from the best, learning is more important than money

We are under extensive pressure now a days to earn as much money as possible in shortest duration of time. This pressure makes us select the easiest ways to reach a stage wherein we can start earning money. In this process, we tend to market whatever skillsets we possess without checking if these skills are half baked or fully developed. Once we get in this rut of earning money, it becomes difficult to focus on improving existing skills or developing new skills. These skillsets does not necessarily be related to professional work only. We can learn new things related to our hobbies, favorite subjects, sports, exercise, entertainment etc.

Easiest way to learn anything, is to learn from the best. Observing, analyzing how the best in the business of life do the things can help us understand their techniques and ways of doing them in an efficient manner. Sometimes, even imitating those helps a lot. The experts in specific fields of interest have already invested a lot of time and energy in honing their skills, they have undergone the complete process of learning and relearning. They are aware of the nuances in the skillset. They can share their experiences with us and we can save a lot of time and energy. It is not easy to find experts in specific fields and making them coach or mentor us, but then efforts to make them agree to help us is a task worthy of investing time in.

Most of the times, money making takes precedence over all the other things in life. Our views become so myopic, that we can only see instant ways of earning money while ignoring long-term views and plans. The abilities and skills which are helping us earn the money now, may not be sufficient enough or sustainable over a long period of time. Instead we can focus on things that can help us reap the benefits over a long period of time. These long term skills sets once built can be continuously used and improved upon while they pay us rich dividends.

Hustle comes first, passion later

A lot of times, we waste time in procrastinating. Delaying things which we understand are important but we are not interested enough to act on it. We keep on waiting till a spark of divine intervention or an angry letter from our boss or client reaches our mailbox.

The point here is we are trying to align our personal interests and passions with the preferences of the tasks that needs to be completed. In our personal and professional lives, not everything can fall in our "Passion" category. We need to work energetically on certain things which are essential for our growth and development. It is completely unnecessary that the essential tasks fall under our "Passion" category. Amazingly enough, while we are hustling in our life, we end up discovering our true passions and interest.

The best way to find out our real passion and not losing time is to start immediately on tasks at hand and work on it with complete focus. We automatically end up getting attracted to things and actions which make us happy and content. Ultimately passions are nothing but a normal work or activity that we really enjoy doing. It is easier to find our passions on the track while we are speeding fast towards the next station, instead of while sitting on the platform waiting for the right train which may be running late.

Internet: the world is flat and democratic

Proliferation of internet is changing the face of the earth. Never in the history of mankind, was knowledge and information so readily and easily available to a vast majority of people. Vast infrastructure built in the last 2-3 decades across the globe has decimated the man-made boundaries and walls which used to prevent a lot of people from accessing information and knowledge to uplift their lives. With Internet, a large section of global population has got direct access to a wealth of knowledge. Internet wave riding on Mobile devices and gadgets is creating even bigger wave of knowledge and information.

Surprisingly enough, even people who are illiterate by common parameters of reading and writing are getting benefitted from the Internet boom. They are easily accessing the video and audio content from Internet at a click of a button. Internet websites and online social groups like YouTube, WhatsApp and Facebook are completely revolutionizing the access to information and communication.

We must take necessary steps to make sure that the Internet/Mobile device wave of Information does not sweep us off our feet. The enormous power of internet can bring us unimaginable damage if not used properly. We must make our children move from online gaming, chatting and surfing to online learning.

Building strong characters

Our total dependence on modern gadgets for basic necessities, controlled parenting, lack of exercise, constant distractions are damaging natural upbringing of children. These unhealthy practices and habits are making our children mentally and physically fragile and weak. They are finding it difficult to interact with people in the real world due to their complete reliance on social networks and online games.

We are losing basic human traits of sportsmanship, creativity and sharing/caring. Children without these basic life skills are failing to withstand external pressures of competition. They are not being able to cope up with even small setbacks in real life. Habits of instant gratification and sense of entitlement are making our children want more and more without putting any efforts to achieve these things. They are getting an impression that everything they want can be achieved just by asking for it. No efforts or hard work is required to achieve these things. Besides many children do not have a robust support system of their grandparents, who used to take care of most of these basic life skills while parents were running breathlessly behind money and careers.

Children are the future of our nation. Self-indulgent, mentally fragile and supremely over-confident children can be a recipe for disaster for us.

Communication for conflict avoidance & conflict resolution

Communication is the most essential skill which plays a very important role throughout our personal and professional lives. Communication is typically considered as a tool for sharing our views and information with each other. Throughout our life, we keep on facing situations wherein, we have to assess our viewpoints and stand up to people with our viewpoints. Understanding other viewpoints and understanding them rationally is an essential skill.

Most of our personal and professional life gets utilized in collaborating with each other on various aspects of life and work. Each individual has his own beliefs and viewpoints.

Bringing everyone together, conveying our thoughts and opinions without creating insecurity and discomfort in others minds and getting things done amicably is the essence of communication.

If we can teach ourselves and our children the art of communication to avoid and resolve conflicts, a lot of time and energy can be saved and utilized for better purposes.

Creativity is the new parameter of literacy

Creativity is the new parameter of literacy. Reading, writing and basic arithmetic are the old ones. Creativity is the ability to think about various possibilities without thinking about making mistakes or being wrong.

All of us have this innate capacity to imaginatively think about various permutations and combinations of possibilities related to certain things or situations or issues or opportunities. When we are not bothered by the fear of being wrong or of making mistakes, we tend to find out multiple ways of handling any kind of problems. Whereas when we are worried about making mistakes and being wrong, we tend to get cautious and apprehensive about finding out new solutions. We end up shutting down our power of imagination. Closed minds can think of mediocre solutions only.

Children are the most creative people because they are not worried about being wrong or about making mistakes. They are not even aware of what a mistake is and what being wrong means. As we grow up, we are programmed to make minimum or no mistakes. Our learning is based on being accurate in everything. This systematic programming of our brains to be accurate every-time, leads us to think within a certain boundary of accuracy and correctness. Over the period of time, we lose the capacity to think creatively.

What can we do about it? We must maintain and nurture our childlike ability to be curious and creative while growing up. The best combination of our strengths of creativity and organized execution is to plan like a child and to execute like an adult.

Current global work-force:

Current global workforce can be largely divided into three main categories. Agricultural and related jobs, Industrial jobs and Services Industry related jobs. The agricultural population can be defined as individuals dependent on agriculture, fishing and forestry. Rest of the industrial and services related jobs include Manufacturing and Production, Office & Administration, Business & Financial Management, Information Technology & Telecommunication, Engineering & Architecture, Legal, Education, Entertainment, Sports, Media, Chemicals, Infrastructure, Oil & Gas, Renewable Energy, Banking, Insurance and Asset Management. Healthcare, Pharmaceuticals, Supply Chain and Transportation, Mining, Automotive etc.

Till 1980s, half of the global working population was involved in Agricultural field and the remaining in Industrial and Services sectors. In the last 35 years, there has been steady decline in the agricultural population from 50% to 38%, whereas industrial and Services employment has increased from 50% to 62%. There is steady decrease going on in the agricultural population across the globe. These numbers needs to be understood in a different context, the world population has almost doubled from 1960 to 2010 from 3 billion to 6.5 billion. Even after explosive growth in the population, comparatively few people are turning towards agriculture. Another important aspect is the growth of agricultural population in Asia and

Africa followed by steady decline in the regions of North, South and Central America with Europe.

Asia and Africa accounts for more than 90% of the global agricultural population, whereas agricultural population in the Americas accounted for less than 4 percent. Productivity of the agricultural population in North America is better compared to other regions due to large scale automation, improved crop varieties, farm machinery, fertilizers/pesticides and irrigation systems.

India had approx. 70% working population involved in agricultural sector in 1950. It has steadily declined to around 45% around 2015. Whereas currently Services sector is supplying jobs to approx. 30% followed closely by Industries catering to 25% of the working population. Even after steady decline in the agricultural workforce, productivity has increased over the period of time due to use of better technology, equipment and farming techniques. When the percentage of human agricultural workforce is declining, the actual number of people involved in agricultural activities is increasing due to population explosion. But this increase in the number of people is not sufficient to take care of the increasing food supply demand.

Looking at the explosion of global population, we are expected to feed population of 9 billion people by 2050. We will have to take care of natural resources while increasing the agricultural production. Pollution of air and water, degradation of soil, greenhouse gas emissions, depleting freshwater supplies are some of the unintended consequences.

Increasing agricultural produce with declining workforce is a serious challenge. In the end, food is the bare minimum necessity of human life. All the industrial and services related progress and development will be of no use, if we cannot feed the people daily. Besides, there is no substitute to farming when it comes to our physical and mental growth requirements. As of now, there are no technological solutions which can substitute our daily intake of food to sustain human bodies.

The non-agricultural population is increasing at almost 3 times that of agricultural population. Industrial and services related jobs are improving lives of millions of people. Their food habits are changing dramatically due to improved financial conditions and availability of variety of food items. The challenge is to sustain the demanding rate of food production rate.

In India, almost 45% working population is involved in activities related to agriculture. Industries related to agriculture are also playing a very important role in employment generation. These industries are food processing industries, farming equipment manufacturing, operations & maintenance, transport, fertilizers, pesticides etc. The farming techniques are improving day by day, which is helping farmers increase the yield and quality of the products.

But there are some teething issues which needs to be taken care of immediately. A vast majority of farmers are involved in traditional methods of agriculture. Most of them are uneducated and illiterate. They have just started getting benefitted from the Internet and its vast knowledge base.

Our traditional methods of agriculture have helped us so far in meeting the food requirement of 6 billion people. The exponential growth in population expected till 2050 and subsequent demand for food cannot be met without bringing in some new innovative ideas of food production.

Since we are primarily focusing on skill sets and employability, we need to understand the Food and Agriculture sector since 30-40% of workforce globally is expected to be employed in agricultural and related sectors.

Complex & interrelated issues

Modern agriculture is the largest consumer of land and fresh water on the planet. It uses approximately 45% of the land and it is the largest consumer of fresh water on the planet, about sixty percent of the world's fresh water consumption is related to conventional agriculture. It is the source of most of the world's water pollution and the major contributor of global greenhouse emissions.

According to official UN estimates our population is going to surpass 9 billion by 2050. Approximately two-thirds of these people are expected to be urban dwellers. That means the agriculture workforce number will be dwindling at a very fast rate whereas the demand for food products will be increasing exponentially.

It also means that once the food is grown and harvested, it needs to be shipped for processing and warehousing. It will be shipped to various locations hundreds if not thousands of kilometers away. Once it reaches the city center, they will be distributed to various stores and people can purchase and consume the same.

This complete lifecycle of food production to consumption by the user puts a lot of pressure on our environmental resources and conditions. Let us consider a scenario wherein, we need to produce a non-vegetarian food. We need animals for the meat. We need farms to raise these animals. These farms are built on natural places once inhabited by a complex ecosystem of flora and fauna. We kill the trees and displace or kill animals and birds in this area to make way for the farm. We use these farms to breed and grow animals whose meat is in high demand in the market. All these animals like goats, cows, pigs, Chicken etc need food to survive and grow.

Since we need these animals to grow quickly and in a healthy manner, we supply good quality food which typically is grains and grass that we either transfer from other parts of the world or grow in the same region/farm. The amount of food grains and water required to produce 1 kg meat or a chocolate or sugar is certainly more than 1 kg of grain or vegetable. These food items can be full of externally added hormones and antibiotics to make the animals grow quickly and stronger. Once these animals are grown, they are slaughtered and transported to various depot locations for distribution and sales using road and air-transport. This method of food production results into rapid deforestation and greenhouse gas emissions. That is Global Warming for us.

Sowing, growing and harvesting are not the only parts of the farming process. Processing, packaging, warehousing, transportation/logistics, sales/marketing are most essential aspects of the modern agriculture. These aspects have commercial and social responsibility angles to it.

Modern agricultural workforce should be able to understand these various aspects of the farming to succeed and survive in the market.

Considering all the above scenarios, if the workforce related to agriculture can be skilled/reskilled to take care of these farm related aspects, coming decades will present one of the biggest opportunities for them to prosper and earn a good life. If we fail to make them ready for the coming global upheaval, this can be extremely frustrating and dangerous period from agro-employment perspective.

To survive and prosper in this demanding market, workforce related to agricultural field must learn new ways of collaborating and engaging with various stakeholders. Communication and team work is going to extremely crucial in this area. Adaptability and creativity to manage the situation and look for innovative solutions can keep us ahead of the competition. Innovative solutions like urban farming, Aquaponics, Hydroponics and Aeroponics are going to be very critical. The traditional farming has limitations of land and other resources. We'll have to look for distributed farming methods of urban farming based on modern technologies.

It will help us reduce transportation and logistics efforts which in turn will reduce carbon footprint. At the same time, locally produced, chemicals free farm produce will be healthier and cost effective. Local and seasonal produce, grown in our own backyards or terraces in controlled environment will be nutritious and healthy. Distributed farming on individual level can completely change quality of the food we consume these days. Large scale deforestation and climate changes can be avoided. Vegetarian diets will also help a lot in controlling global warming.

Farming has been the most basic and critical aspect of our growth as a human race. We have made tremendous progress based on the ability of the agricultural sector's capacity to satiate global food demand continuously for thousands of years.

Situation is changing very fast. We'll have to skill and reskill farmers to think about building innovative, cost-effective, nature friendly and good quality agricultural products in shortest production cycles.

We have discussed health epidemics in the previous chapter. While we are racing towards developing advanced cutting edge technology in all spheres of life, we cannot afford to ignore basic human needs of food. Neither can we afford to leave behind the less fortunate people who are being relegated to sidelines of the Life Express due to their lack of access to basic education and extreme poverty.

Rapid deforestation and global climatic changes are making large swathes of land unproductive in a very short period of time. Besides, land available for agriculture is limited. Not everybody can have access to land. Production of food items on industrial scale, is unfortunately marred by vested financial & business interests. Being under pressure to earn a lot of money in shortest possible time, these companies are focusing on quantity and availability rather than quality and easy access to food. Understandably, industrial houses are focused on earning profits to keep their shareholders happy, but critical point is to understand where to stop so that people don't end up consuming food which is unhealthy owing to widespread usage of hormones, antibiotics, pesticides, herbicides and fertilizers. Business interests of earning easy money is shadowing their social awareness & corporate responsibility initiatives. Large industrial farming complexes are contributing to global warming and pollution too due to transport and logistics requirements.

The new age farmer needs to be educated, made aware and trained in overcoming these difficulties. Besides having knowledge of traditional farming methods, he'll have to develop different skillsets of communication, information gathering, understanding of sales and marketing of his produce as per continuously changing food habits and market conditions.

Rapid urbanization and continuous erosion of value in the farming business, is creating a crisis situation for famers and agricultural workers. Their crops are heavily dependent on weather conditions. If the weather is good, farmers end up yielding bumper crops, the facilities of processing this raw produce and warehousing are very limited. Transportation and logistics costs are prohibitive. Market values of the crops are not controlled by farmers and consumers but by the middleman and traders. Consumers end up paying more and farmers end up getting very less profits. Most of the profits are pocketed by traders and middlemen. Most of the time, farmers are helpless due to lack of understanding of the sales process and multiple options available for selling besides exploitation by transportation services and traders.

Due to continuous fall in income levels, almost all the farmers are preventing their children from getting into farming. They are educating them for better jobs and improved lifestyle. A huge number of people are moving from villages to nearest cities and towns to earn their living by abandoning their farming profession. It is a very scary situation. We'll have to take care of our farmers and improve their skillsets and our approach towards farming. The most effective way of doing it will be to involve ourselves in farming activities in whatever possible way. We can start working with farmers by training them about communication and market information or by growing small amounts of vegetables in our urban houses.

Urban farming can take care of a lot of problems at a very small scale. Quality of the food we consume can be controlled. We can select from the variety of food items to grow in our terrace garden. It helps reduce stress and improves wellbeing. Needs of mass transportation and logistics can be avoided resulting into reduced carbon footprint. Use of land and deforestation can be controlled by using methods like hydroponics or Aquaponics.

Modern technology can play a very important role in improving constantly deteriorating situation of farmers.

We'll have to focus on these issues and take corrective actions immediately. Any delay in this regard has the potential to nullify the technological and other advances we may make in the future, if people do not have healthy food to consume.

Some of the skills which can benefit farmers in their daily lives are:

1. Creating and maintaining self-help and similar interest groups on social networks. Cost effective Internet penetration is certainly helping farmers get knowledge and information about various trends about market prices. They can very easily seek guidance from the experts and share their experiences and views on various topics. This easy method of online information sharing can help a lot.

2. Improving farmers' knowledge about financial matters is one of the biggest need of the hour. Lack of formal education and basic understanding of handling money is creating one of the biggest socio-economic problem. Farmers are committing suicides owing to their inability to manage finances and stress caused due to bad crops and financial difficulties. Imparting basic life skills of financial management, Motivation and general knowledge of new farming techniques can certainly help them maintain their physical and mental health resulting into better outcomes from the farming practice.

3. Farmers are always very close to natural resources. Under continuously changing market conditions and natural threats like famines, floods, global warming etc, we will have to help them understand critical role of natural resources and their limited availability. Managing and utilizing them in a better manner can help us a lot in maintaining natural balance. Generally farmers' awareness and sensitivity towards natural resources is far better compared to their urban and educated

counterparts. They may be not be aware about their holistic role in the growth and sustenance of the mankind.

4. Once the crops are harvested, farmers face the biggest difficulty in selling their produce and negotiating better prices. Basic understanding of marketing skills and negotiation tactics can help a lot. Awareness about the complete product lifecycle of food items can also help them in approaching new prospects and clients directly instead of sharing profits with middleman and traders. Knowledge of sales/marketing, packaging, transportation and product delivery is essential to achieve better margins.

5. Looking for new ways of improving the production and optimum utilization of natural resources can reduce farmers' dependency on changing and unpredictable nature patterns. Innovative solutions will also keep them ahead of the competition.

Presenteeism, absenteeism in life & workplace

Presenteeism and Absenteeism are the terms used in modern workplaces to identify lack of complete attention to assigned work due to various reasons like illness, poor benefits, personal issues, nagging and undertrained supervisors along with other personal or professional reasons.

To understand these concepts in detail, we need to understand some basic ideas about employee-employer relationship. The basic understanding between an employee and the employer is that employer will pay employee a certain amount i.e. salary against the completion of specific task or work as per the requirements specified by the employer within specific timeframe so that the organization grows financially. Under normal circumstances, it being humane interaction, employees tend to get certain leeway in finishing their tasks as per their convenience. Mutual trust and understanding between company supervisors and management with the employee plays a very important part in this mutually beneficial relationship.

This relationship tends to get strained when one of them starts deviating from their intended goals and objectives i.e. functional outcomes. Organization may put additional pressure and workload on an employee or an employee may start wasting time and company resources without finishing the intended tasks within stipulated time.

Presenteeism and Absenteeism ideas are typically applied to employees. Let us understand the meaning and its effects on personal and professional wellbeing and growth.

Presenteeism

Presenteeism basically refers to a condition wherein an employee attends the office but is not working with complete attention and focus or is facing difficulties while performing normal tasks at work. Presenteeism does not refer to the acts like taking extended tea and lunch breaks, surfing internet for personal reasons, pretending to be ill to avoid working etc. Presenteeism refers to the condition wherein real mental or physical health issues of an employee are resulting into loss of productivity of an individual and hence his department. The health issues can be mental depression, stress, allergies, chronic back pain etc. Typically when these health problems are not severe, employees tend to report for duty but cannot work with complete focus and attention.

The mental or health related issues can have various effects on the capacity of an individual to perform intended tasks. These employees may have certain activity limitations due to illnesses or mental issues like depression or anxiety. They fail to complete certain activity which is an essential part of the task assigned to them.

Absenteeism

Absenteeism refers to being absent from the workplace during work-hours. The employee may be taking long tea and lunch breaks, he may be out for shopping during working hours, he may be absent without leave. The important point in absenteeism is that the employee intends to return to work. He is not leaving his job, but is not dedicating completely towards the task at hand. This condition results into huge productivity loss to the company, since we are not being able to utilize employee's services towards completing various projects and tasks assigned to him or her. The reasons behind absenteeism can be health issues or job dissatisfaction or attitude problems or work related burnouts.

For the growth and development of an organization, handling these issues of Presenteeism and absenteeism are very important. These issues can spread like wildfire in the organization if not tackled efficiently and urgently. It can destroy company work cultures.

Effects of presenteeism and absenteeism in life

These issues can be considered as barometers of the health conditions and its effects on individuals and companies. These can be used to ascertain the extent of how health problems are affecting the normal functioning or professional & social tasks of an individual. The idea of Presenteeism and absenteeism is relevant to our personal lives as well.

In our personal lives, we are responsible for our social conduct, our relationships with family members, friends, neighbors, colleagues and other society members. These responsibilities can be divided in three general categories, Personal, Social and Financial. Personal responsibilities are towards our family, taking care of their development and growth. Social responsibilities include our abiding by the societal norms and contribution towards the development and growth of our society. Financial responsibility is to earn a living by tendering our services to companies or organizations or social institutes. This earning can be used for taking care of our day to day needs and wants.

Most of us typically follow all these guidelines about personal and social responsibility. Ever-changing workplace and social dynamics are putting enormous pressure on us daily. Our food habits are changing dramatically, our exercise routines are going for a toss. Competition and race to own more and more materialistic possessions is putting us in continuous stress condition. Pressure to earn more and more money to satiate never ending material needs and wants are making us neglect our health and relationships. We are not able to find any time for family and ourselves due to our busy schedules. Hence we are victims of Presenteeism and Absenteeism issues.

Presenteeism in our personal lives is our tendency to not being able to take good care of our job as a father, brother, sister, mother or children. Our daily routines and work related issues are creating mental and physical health problems for ourselves. We are in no condition to take care of our personal relationships any more. We are failing in taking sound financial decisions most of the time. We are physically present with the family but are mentally adrift in our own thoughts and fancies. We have started using our homes as a lodging & boarding place. Our emotional and mental absence in our home or in our family is creating a lot of problems for our near and dear ones.

Absenteeism related to our personal lives is our lack of willingness to actively participate in the games our children are playing. It is our tendency to spend as much time as possible in keeping us distracted from our personal lives using different gadgets and other modes of constant source of irrelevant information and knowledge. Absenteeism is our tendency to hide our issues and problems from our family members. Reasons can be anything. We may think about not sharing our problems with our family to avoid making them uncomfortable or we may think about not bothering them with your issues so that they can be happy. Our objectives behind hiding our issues and problems can be many, but our relationships and families are suffering due to our constant state of frustration, despair and silent distress.

These symptoms must be diagnosed and treated as soon as possible. These two eism's makes us suffer in our personal and professional lives. It results into our poor time management. We fail to stay organized and composed in critical situations. It starts affecting our interpersonal relationships. It starts affecting our ability to help each other and our ability to collaborate with others to achieve common goals and objectives. Constant distractions and physical/mental exhaustion results into our failure to complete simple routine tasks successfully. We keep on delaying action on matters of urgency. Our complete skillsets and organization of daily routines/activities gets badly hampered due to our part present and part absent lifestyle.

Our Virtual Presence and Real Absence from our workplace or from our family affects not only our personal lives but also collective performance of our colleagues, team members and organization. It also affects personal lives of our near and dear ones. They can feel our discomfort and agony, but they cannot help us due to our stonewalling. Our capacity to manage our tasks gets seriously hampered. We get extremely annoyed at the slightest hint of any change in our surroundings or work conditions. Adaptability and collaboration abilities take a backseat. We get very easily distracted by external things happening around us. We fail to finish our tasks due to lack of concentration. We lose our critical thinking and problem solving capacity. All these negative emotions starts overpowering us. We start feeling cheated and treated unfairly by others. We start getting isolated and disconnected from our comforting hobbies, friends and family. We end up feeling miserable, disinterested and demotivated. It all ends up into our failure in relationships and professional assignments.

All these issues can be diagnosed very early and can be taken care of by conscious efforts by us with the help of our family members and colleagues.

One very important distinction between absenteeism in Work and absenteeism in personal life is the cause behind it. In Professional lives, absenteeism can be caused by sore relationship with your boss or job dissatisfaction or bad working conditions or low pay or unfair treatment in the office etc. In personal life absenteeism, our family members have no clue about our condition. We are absent in our personal lives due to work pressure, distractions, addictions, stress, depression, anxiety, financial burdens and our inability to cope with them.

IQ: a double edged sword

Intelligence quotient is used as a parameter of gauging ones intelligence based on a set of standardized test questions. The IQ we are discussing in this chapter is not the Intelligence Quotient but it is our Ignorance Quotient.

Ignorance basically is a lack of knowledge, understanding and awareness. Ignorance is a state wherein we tend to have no knowledge or awareness of important things happening around us, things that can have huge impact on our lives.

Ignorance typically has a negative connotation. Being called ignorant is offensive to many people. It means stupidity, carelessness, lack of attention, being unaware, uninformed and misled in some cases. All these negative feelings attached to state of ignorance is not the complete picture. Ignorance can be conscious or intentional. Ignorance doesn't have to be negative every time. It can be used in a positive sense to understand and accept that we are unaware of certain things and to take necessary actions to make ourselves knowledgeable in these previously ignored areas.

Ignorance is power & knowledge is bliss

Let us assume that we have worked hard and have gained enormous knowledge about certain aspects of life. We are happy, blissful and proud about this knowledge. At the same time we are very keenly aware of the fact that there are so many unanswered questions about this particular aspect which needs to be worked upon, which needs to be answered. This inquisitive nature of always being aware of our ignorance supplemented by our innate eagerness to find those solutions is a power.

Being constantly aware of our ignorance towards so many things in life, our unquenchable thirst to find out answers to the numerous questions arising out of this lack of knowledge & clarity has constantly helped us better our lives and human existence over thousands of years.

We are designed to be curious and inquisitive by nature. Our brains are programmed to continuously scan our surroundings for opportunities and dangers. We are primitively programmed to gather information, process the information and categorize the information under food or threat category. Reproduction, survival and food were the main objective of human life. We made progress by keenly observing and analyzing our situations, modulating our responses and reactions to these situations. We were able to use brain for more advanced processing and decision making by deferring our "Fight or Flight" responses.

Throughout our journey of evolution, one constant aspect which has helped us strive for superior life experiences and comforts is our ability to nurture our eagerness and adapt to different situations by learning and relearning various life skills.

We are in this amazing state of never noticing what has already been done, but of focusing on what remains to be done. Everything that has been accomplished is understated and all our focus and energy is concentrated on what needs to be achieved to further our progress and existence.

Our focus on what needs to be done is based on our conscious understanding of our lack of awareness i.e. ignorance towards certain things or aspects which needs to be worked upon, which needs to be built upon. This constant urge to find new paradigms of life has helped us move from hunter-gatherer to form farming colonies, to learn about lighting up fire, to make weapons from stones and wood, to develop family structures, to hunt in a team, to protect ourselves from natural calamities, to keep ourselves safe and safeguard our families, to communicate with each other etc. These primitive skills of life are direct result of our consistent observation, our sense of lack of awareness and our keen willingness to understand the unknown.

All our scientific inventions and technical breakthroughs are the direct result of our conscious efforts towards understanding and accepting our ignorance levels. Once we understand the areas we are ignorant about, it becomes easy to focus on these areas and improve or work upon those areas. Ignorance becomes power, when we understand our lack of awareness about certain things and aspects of life. It is the power which helps us summon all our resources towards finding out possible solutions in our areas of ignorance. With this powerful focus on problems, we can utilize our existing knowledge and ideas for finding out ways and means of overcoming the loopholes created by ignorance. Hence awareness of ignorance is a power which propels us to look beyond the current achievements and to strive to improve upon prevalent measures of knowledge and success.

Acceptance of our ignorance related to flying like birds, led our scientists and people like Wright Brothers to look for various methods and techniques which could make a man fly using airplanes. Acceptance of our ignorance towards depletion of natural fuel resources lead us to develop solar energy systems. Our acceptance of ignorance related to common platform of easiest knowledge sharing on a global scale, led us to Internet. Millions and millions of us can now use internet to share and gather information on any subject from any part of the world.

Hence awareness of our ignorance levels is the power which can be help us look for possible solutions using our existing knowledge as a foundation.

Knowledge is power & ignorance is bliss

If we are satisfied with the knowledge that whatever we have achieved so far is the end of it all and there is nothing more left to be done in the life, then the knowledge we have acquired is a power. Having no idea or willingness to understand what else can be done or what else needs to be done, is a blissful ignorance.

Our capacity to understand, store and process information on such a complex level differentiates us from other animals. Our brains supported by our senses, help us survive, prosper, think, learn adapt and innovate. We are acquiring all the knowledge around us depending on our individual capacities and preferences. We are trying to achieve our goals and objectives using available knowledge and information.

For most of us, leading our lives based on knowledge or information available is sufficient. We are happy and content with our present status. Being completely oblivious from any additional needs and wants is basic state of ignorance. This state of accomplishment with present knowledge is powerful enough for us. In this state of mind, we are powerful with the knowledge we have and are blissful about our ignorance.

An example of powerfully knowledgeable and blissfully ignorant state of mind can be our citizenry. Most of the common citizens are very happy, content and confident about the knowledge and information they gather, store and process. All of the life decisions are based on the knowledge acquired in this manner. On the other hand, there always is a group of people who drives the public discourse of seemingly infinite knowledge and information sources. This group decides, what information can be made publically neavailable kand what the popular public opinions can be. They manipulate, subvert the information in such a way that it suits their personal/ political/social/religious agendas. Common populace gets high on the knowledge made selectively available to them. They gather all this information, process it and reach to pre-fixed conclusions which are in line with the manipulators' agendas. In this example, citizenry has powerful knowledge but they are blissfully ignorant about the veracity and authenticity of the information.

Second relevant example can be our education system. We are making our children attend modern schools and colleges with complete faith that they will impart all the knowledge and education to our wards. Our wards will be ready for their personal and professional lives. Our educational institutes are not to be blamed for this. They are doing everything possible to educate our children in the best possible way. This is one side of the story about the knowledge empowering us to lead our lives in a more meaningful way. The other side of the story related to blissful ignorance is mismatch between the things taught to children and expectations of the market, industries and day today life from them. The expectations of the market and industries from their potential employees are changing at a very fast rate. These expectations are not getting fulfilled which is resulting into unemployment. Unemployment is not because of lack of resources, it is because of lack of employability of these resources. The education and knowledge acquired is proving to be insufficient to lead our personal lives in a better way because basic life skills are missing from the education. Neither parents nor schools are imparting life skill knowledge to students. While we are complacent about our acquired education and knowledge, we are blissfully ignorant about our employability and our life skills levels.

Controlled Neglect to avoid stress and wastage of resources. We can take informed calls on neglecting some of the aspects instead of completely ignoring them. We just don't have to worry about it. Knowing a lot of stuff is important in any field. Knowing a lot of stuff is not sufficient, knowing a lot of stuff to generate even more questions and possibilities in our minds should be the real intention of knowledge and education.

Knowledge should not be limited to solving a puzzle. With the puzzles, generally answers are already defined and available. We just have to find out the right answer or match with the right answer to solve the puzzle. The real lack of solution awareness should make us use our knowledge to unravel new solutions to existing or new puzzles. That is a real differentiator. Our education systems are training us to solve puzzles with prefixed answers. We are not motivated to find new solutions to existing puzzles, because these new solutions doesn't match with the prefixed answers and we might end up failing in the examinations. Neither are we inspired to create new puzzles.

Knowledge and awareness about ignorance are blissfully powerful

Ignorance is one of the biggest issues we are facing today. Constant information deluge and energy wasted in scanning & processing this information is making us shut down our observation about things happening around us. We are becoming oblivious to important aspects of our lives and simple enjoyable things present around us.

We have started ignoring our health conditions. We are so engrossed in our daily lives and material achievements that we are failing to take good care of our body and mind. We are so busy these days that we are not able to spend any time in exercising our body and brain. We are paying no attention to the distress signals our bodies and our minds are sending us. These signals are calling for immediate action to avoid certain situations or circumstances which are creating uncomfortable health conditions. These signals are calling for immediate steps towards keeping our mind and brain active and alert all the times.

We are ignoring our families and their emotional needs. We are so busy in our professions that we cannot find any time to spend with our children and families. They are growing up without our active participation in their lives. Arranging money for education and other hobbies is a small portion of complete upbringing of our children. Our ignorance towards child development is creating a lot of problems for the children who are looking for our help and guidance in learning new things.

We are ignoring our financial matters till the time we end up paying huge penalty for the ignorance and lack of awareness. Working for making money and making money work for us are two very different things. We are ending up working for making money throughout our lives. Our objectives are to earn as much money as possible in the shortest period of time, so that our children and families can lead happy and luxurious lives. Unfortunately earning money part of the problem is sapping all our energy and resources, we are reaching our homes completely exhausted and frustrated.

We are ignoring our social needs of helping each other. We have innate willingness to participate in various social activities. We are ready to contribute to society progress and development but lack of time and energy is making it difficult to pay any attention to these aspects.

One more aspect of ignorance is extremely dangerous. Sometimes people use ignorance as a tool to not accept situations and conditions that are not favorable to them. Instead of accepting the uncomfortable truths, they take help of the ignorance tool and behave as if they are not even aware of those circumstances or events. Politicians use this tool regularly. If accepting global warming threat is not beneficial to us, we will completely ignore the topic as if we have absolutely no idea about what the global warming is. This is classic case of selective ignorance.

Unfortunately our ignorance quotient is increasing day by day, resulting into more and more frustration and degraded lifestyles across the society. We are becoming insensitive towards important social and personal issues and problems. Most of the issues and problems are ignored by stating that the problem is not mine. It is somebody else's issue and I should not waste my time and energy on resolving the same. We are basically postponing the inevitability of the issue reaching our doorstep one or the other day. Global issues of drug addiction and water conservation are some of the examples of our ignorance and careless attitude.

The real question is not "How much I know about something" but "What question can I ask about something I know?" We need to have great knowledge but the purpose of a lot of knowledge is not to have a lot of knowledge but to ask a lot of questions about the knowledge we have, to ask more and more interesting and thought provoking questions. This is how we can continuously enhance our knowledge, frame new questions based on our enhanced knowledge and find new solutions to these newly formed questions.. the cycle repeats itself.

Some of the random questions I have, based on my limited knowledge are about our intuitions, our dreams, our bodies, our mind and our ability of self-destruction.

I am fascinated by how our intuition works?

How it preempts us about the future threats and possibilities?

How our dreams are created?

Who decides the topic of the dreams?

How can we have a complete cinematic experience without retakes, editing and special effects?

How can our minds roam around seamlessly from one thought to another without following session termination and session initiation? If they are following these protocols, what are the timeframes for the session initiation and termination?

How the human body is so efficient on Energy to weight ratio?

How can we replicate such a complex but seamless functioning of various machine parts without compromising on energy intake and power output?

Is it possible to improve on the already optimized human bodies so that they can perform superhuman tasks like flying or becoming invisible or teleportation?

Just like machines, why can't human beings have redundant critical functions like heart and brain?

Can we have a 100% part replacement policy for critical organs of our bodies?

Just like intelligent softwares, can human bodies have enhanced self-healing properties?

Can we develop a graphic user interface for our brain wherein we can monitor and control brain functions?

Can we terminate resource intensive sessions of the brain with a click of a button?

Can we allocate limited amount of brain resources for certain activities & feelings like procrastination and arrogance?

Can we improve common sense and civic sense in an individual by a single click of a button?

Can we restart our complete body functions?

Can we format our brain drives and install new ones?

What will happen if we can find a modular solution of learning wherein we can choose subjects of our choice and install those modules in our brains instantly? Like for example, I want to learn Quantum Mechanics, I can straight away purchase Quantum Mechanics pack in Marathi language with all the colorful fonts and install it into my system in 2 minutes without upgrading my RAM or Harddrive?

I understand, there will be unintended repercussions about it all, but there is nothing wrong in asking questions? People typically are very insecure about such out of box questions. Nobody likes to be branded uninformed or uneducated or plain stupid. Large groups of people oppose any new thought processes which can question their knowledge and set thought patterns. They fight such innovative ideas tooth and nail until they are forced to accept new path breaking realities. Irrespective of such opposition, some of us are already working on these lines. Let us hope for the best.

There are so many senseless and illogical questions related to many fields and subjects which keep bothering me from time to time.

The most optimum utilization of our knowledge and our awareness about ignorance is in striving for finding solutions to our areas of ignorance by building on our current knowledge. Once we find new answers to our questions, some more questions will crop up, we'll keep on finding new solutions and new questions and the continuous cycle of creating and solving our problems will lead us to further our amazing journey of progress and prosperity.

Knowledge and Ignorance needs to be in symbiotic relationship. More the knowledge, more the awareness of ignorance. More the awareness of ignorance, more the search for solutions and knowledge. That is the way we have prospered for the last thousands of years and this is the way we can break all the technological, social, political and personal barriers for thousands of years to come.

Most essential basic life skills

As per our ancient life education system, we had 64 kalas (performing arts) and 14 Vidyas (Techniques) which used to cover almost all the aspects of the human life. We could choose the arts we were interested in and then could learn the art from the masters by living with them in their home or ashram.

The most important part of this education system is the choice of selection of learning the art was with the student. Each student used to decide art of his interest and liking. Most of the time, these art forms were selected depending on the profession families used to be in. Experienced professional in the family used to guide their children in learning these arts. This is how information and intrinsic knowledge used to pass from one generation to the next generation.

Let us have a look at these 64 arts.

1. Geet vidya — art of singing.

2. Vadya vidya —art of playing on musical instruments.

3. Nritya vidya — art of dancing.

4. Natya Vidya — art of theatricals.

5. Alekhya Vidya — art of painting.

6. Viseshakacchedya Vidya — art of painting the face and body with color

7. Tandula-Kusuma-Bali-Vikara — art of preparing offerings from rice and flowers.

8. Pushpastarana — art of making a covering of flowers for a bed.

9. Dasana-Vasananga-Raga — art of applying preparations for cleansing the teeth, cloths and painting the body.

10. Mani-Bhumika-Karma — art of making the groundwork of jewels.

11. Sayya-Rachana — art of covering the bed.

12. Udaka-Vadya — art of playing on music in water.

13. Udaka-Ghata — art of splashing with water.

14. Chitra-Yoga — art of practically applying an admixture of colors.

15. Malya-Grathana-Vikalpa — art of designing a preparation of wreaths.

16. Sekharapida-Yojana — art of practically setting the coronet on the head.

17. Nepathya-Yoga — art of practically dressing in the tiring room.

18. Karnapatra-Bhanga — art of decorating the tragus of the ear.

19. Sugandha-Yukti — art of practical application of aromatics.

20. Bhushana-yojana — art of applying or setting ornaments.

21. Aindra-Kala — art of juggling.

22. Kaucumara — a kind of art.

23. Hasta-Laghava — art of sleight of hand.

24. Citra-Sakapupa-Bhakshya-Vikara-Kriya — art of preparing varieties of delicious food.

25. Panaka-Rasa-Ragasava-Yojana — art of practically preparing palatable drinks and tinging draughts with red color.

26. Suci-Vaya-Karma — art of needleworks and weaving.

27. Sutra-Krida — art of playing with thread.

28. Vina-Damuraka-Vadya — art of playing on lute and small drum.

29. Prahelika — art of making and solving riddles.

30. Durvacaka-yoga — art of practicing language difficult to be answered by others.

31. Pustaka-Vachana — art of reciting books.

32. Natikakhyayika-Darsana — art of enacting short plays and anecdotes.

33. Kavya-Samasya-Purana — art of solving enigmatic verses.

34. Pattika-Vetra-Bana-Vikalpa — art of designing preparation of shield, cane and arrows.

35. Tarku-Karma — art of spinning by spindle.

36. Takshana — art of carpentry.

37. Vastu-Vidya — art of engineering.

38. Raupya-Ratna-Pariksha — art of testing silver and jewels.

39. Dhatu-Vada — art of metallurgy.

40. Mani-Raga Jnana — art of tinging jewels.

41. Akara Jnana — art of mineralogy.

42. Vrikshayur-Veda-Yoga — art of practicing medicine or medical treatment, by herbs.

43. Mesha-Kukkuta-Lavaka-Yuddha-Vidhi — art of knowing the mode of fighting of lambs, cocks and birds.

44. Suka-Sarika-Prapalana (pralapana) — art of maintaining or knowing conversation between male and female cockatoos.

45. Utsadana — art of healing or cleaning a person with perfumes.

46. Kesa-Marjana-Kausala — art of combing hair.

47. Akshara-Mushtika-Kathana — art of talking with fingers.

48. Dharana-Matrika — art of the use of amulets.

49. Desa-Bhasha-Jnana — art of knowing provincial dialects.

50. Nirmiti-Jnana — art of knowing prediction by heavenly voice

51. Yantra-Matrika — art of mechanics.

52. Mlecchita-Kutarka-Vikalpa — art of fabricating barbarous or foreign sophistry.

53. Samvacya — art of conversation.

54. Manasi Kavya-Kriya — art of composing verse mentally.

55. Kriya-Vikalpa — art of designing a literary work or a medical remedy.

56. Chalitaka-Yoga — art of practicing as a builder of shrines called after him.

57. Abhidhana-Kosha-Cchando-Jnana — art of the use of lexicography and meters.

58. Vastra-Gopana — art of concealment of cloths.

59. Dyuta-Visesha — art of knowing specific gambling.

60. Akarsha-Krida — art of playing with dice or magnet.

61. Balaka-Kridanaka — art of using children's toys.

62. Vainayiki Vidya — art of enforcing discipline.

63. Vaijayiki Vidya — art of gaining victory.

64. Vaitaliki Vidya — art of awakening master with music at dawn

Some of these arts are no longer relevant considering evolved lifestyles and the role technologies are playing in our daily lives. But still many of the above mentioned arts are very significant considering our overdependence on technical tools and gadgets in our daily lives.

Let us have a look at some important skills which are essential to lead a successful and healthy life.

1. Having awareness of the world around us, observing things happening around us. Analyzing those events and drawing our own conclusions. Checking these conclusions against the reality and learning from the mistakes made.

2. Working consciously towards making rational decisions about food, exercise, rest and the way we use our energy in order to live a healthy and content life

3. Thinking through various options to solve our problems and issues. Considering every action and its possible repercussions before executing them. Taking responsibility of all our actions and their consequences.

4. Handling ourselves and taking care of our dependents safety while living in the complex world.

5. Taking well informed decisions based on thorough understanding of the issues and their possible solutions. Considering our current strengths and future prospects should be the biggest parameters behind taking life decisions.

6. Understanding various aspects of life such as honor, integrity, loyalty, ethics, morality, love, greed, hatred, independence etc. and relating these aspects with our day to day actions by practicing good ones and banishing bad ones.

7. Choosing relevant education stream, which matches with our interest levels and at the same time helps us standup in the society and be counted as an important contributor to the well-being of the society while earning livelihood.

8. Managing cheerful persona and attracting like-minded people. Everybody faces tough situations and problems. We can spread happiness and peace, if we can behave gracefully and

cheerfully with everybody around us. Happiness is a contagious emotion. It spreads very easily.

9. Always keeping positive attitude towards every situation. It helps us keeping our mind open to various possible solutions to the calamities and issues. Negative thoughts can cloud our rational thinking and problem solving capacity.

10. Keeping our behavior in line with the set goals and objectives within socially accepted norms. These behavioral patterns (habits) can have a major impact on our day to day life.

11. Developing keen sense of taking calculated risks to achieve intended results while being aware of exit options and ways and means of taking advantage of the situations.

12. Stopping being a Garbage truck carrying waste everywhere in life. Focusing on solutions instead of thinking about problems helps us find better solutions. We must avoid wasting our precious energy in thinking about issues and problems. Nothing can be achieved by thinking about problems, easiest way out is to find solutions to these issues.

13. Look at our life from a third person's perspective helps a lot. It helps us see small issues in the larger perspective. We tend to get embroiled in our daily problems and issues and fail to take a long term view of the situations. Most of the daily problems we face do not have any significant effect on our long term success. Hence those should be handled without putting ourselves under stress.

14. Making necessary changes in our daily routines or decision making helps us a lot. Being flexible and accommodative to other viewpoints and opinions can help us find better solutions to our issues without hurting others.

15. Being aware and sensitive to needs and wants of others makes us take mutually beneficial actions. It helps spread happiness and sense of belonging with others.

16. Keen awareness of what makes us happy is one of the most important aspect of life we are missing almost completely. We can literally note down the things which makes us happy and keep on repeating them on a regular basis. We'll be surprised at how simple things can give us so much pleasure and happiness. We need to be in touch with our regular happiness dose.

17. Accepting the life situations is the best way of managing them. Confronting these situations which are beyond our control results into nothing and we end up feeling defeated and exhausted. A lot of heartache and energy can be saved if we can gracefully accept the life situations and focus on making the best of these circumstances.

18. Life is full of people of different characters and personalities. All of us are unique in our own way. There will always be different viewpoints and opinions about everything. We will have to accept the chaotic nature of human interactions. In the end, every bad situation opens up new opportunities and possibilities. We need to focus on these new opportunities which manifest themselves under some unfortunate circumstances.

19. Having the grit to accept the mistakes and the ability to take corrective actions is one the most important skill.

20. Most importantly, having an open mind without being judgmental and biased with preconceived notions about things or situations helps us take a balanced view of the life situations.

21. We are social animals. We have to interact with many people on daily basis for different reasons. It is critical to respect others with their strengths and weaknesses. Interactions can be

fruitful only when objectives of all the parties involved can be taken care of.

22. Building real social networks is extremely important. Though it is extremely difficult to master this art, we will have to make concerted efforts to build a strong network of people from all the walks of life.

23. Maintaining relationships with superiors and authorities is an essential skill. The way we interact with the authorities, the way we share information, the way in which we seek guidance from them, the way in which we help them achieve their objectives goes a long way in building strong relationship. There can be occasions when we may have to question the authorities. There are ways and means of presenting our objections and doubts in front of them. We should not hurt their egos and sentiments by behaving in arrogant and aggressive manner. Though questioning or not following authorities' orders can give us a momentary high of Rebellion, in the long term, it damages our personal and professional prospects.

24. Being a responsible citizen of a free country, we have certain responsibilities and rights accorded to us. It is critical to understand our responsibilities towards the nation and the society before standing up for our rights. Rights without responsibilities results into total chaos and havoc in the society.

25. Our social behavior must follow socially accepted norms and etiquettes. Especially while in public places, we need to be extra careful about not causing discomfort to others due to our brash behavior.

26. Nobody can be perfect in all the aspects of life. We will have to respect others with their strengths and weaknesses. Together we can build on our strengths and work on our weaknesses.

27. Motivating others, encouraging them to achieve their goals and helping them when they need our help is the best way of becoming a worthy member of a society. Society needs good role models who can inspire and guide others.

28. There is no solution for avoiding all the problems in our life. We must face them squarely. The best way to approach any difficulty or problem is to understand the issue first, analyzing the reasons behind the creation of the problem, finding out various possible solutions to the problem and most importantly selecting the best possible solution after considering all the pros and cons of the solution.

29. There will always be many challenges and problems in front of us. Understanding the cost and value of solving or not solving the problem is very important. Some problems don't deserve to be solved, we can always bypass them or ignore them. Wasting our precious time and energy on solving irrelevant problems can be avoided. Critical factor is to make an informed decision about whether to tackle the problem head on or to ignore it by taking other routes.

30. Making wrong commitments are the biggest mistakes. We should make sure that whatever commitments we are making, we should honor them under any circumstances. Leaving the other person or party high and dry just because you don't want to honor your commitments is not a good idea. Our name and personal value deteriorates very quickly. People stop believing in us and our commitments. It is very easy to lose face, but it takes a lot of time and efforts to earn good reputation.

31. Being aware of our own strengths and weaknesses helps us focus on executing the task at hand. It helps us focus on our areas of expertise.

32. Being a sincere, hardworking, ethical and result oriented person or employee always helps us earn a good living which

can provide for adequate food, clothing, education, shelter and medical care for ourselves and our families.

33. Most of the times, the reaction to our communication with others depends on the way in which we share our thoughts, opinions, feelings and ideas with others. If the tone of our voice and our body language are correct, people will listen to our points and will react accordingly. All of us have a tendency of reacting to the communication in the exact same tone and tenor.

34. We are different from animals. We are an intelligent species. Fulfilling our physical needs is basic skill that all the animals possess. We are different from other animals in the sense of our evolved way of leading our lives. We have social needs, aspirational needs besides physical needs. We strive to achieve these needs like social status and success. It is therefore critical to understand who we are and what are our strengths? Based on these strengths, what can we do in our life? And how can we excel in the field of our choice?

35. Self-awareness of our interests and passions, our potential can help us plan our journey in the life. Building on our passions and strengths can help us achieve lofty goals in our lives. These goals can be achieved by focusing on our objectives and solutions while avoiding wasting time on diversions and distractions.

Let us add some important practical skills which are essential to survive daily routines without depending on others.

36. Cooking Skill is an essential skill. There can be occasions when we will have to prepare our food due to whatever reasons like family out of town or restaurants closed due to some reasons. It is always better to cook our own food. By doing so, we can control all the ingredients in the food. We can prepare

food of our choice. Cooking is a good stress buster. We can experiment with cooking. We don't have to be a master chef. We can practice 2-3 dishes and master them to survive on our own for some days at least.

37. Learning to use kitchen appliances can also help us survive for a day or two without any help. Juicers, toasters, microwave ovens and pressure cookers are some of the easy to use kitchen appliances. We can very easily learn to use them.

38. Basic housekeeping skills are very necessary to maintain our house neat, clean and hygienic.

39. Basic Home Repairs is a major task now a days. Trained personnel who can take care of routine home repairs like plumbing and electric connections are not available most of the time. Besides if they are available, they end up turning 24 hours after calling them. Basic home repair jobs can be done ourselves. Basic plumbing and electrical jobs including fixing lightbulbs, repairing leaky faucets and cleaning showers regularly can be taken care of very easily.

40. Public speaking is an essential new age life skill. Stage fright is a very common phenomena. Many people fear the prospect of public speaking. They immediately leave the place where there is a chance for them to be called upon stage. It is a very important platform to share our views and feelings with a lot of people at the same time. We must learn and practice public speaking from early age.

41. Effective communication for conflict avoidance and conflict resolutions is the most critical life skill. Communication to convey our feelings, views and messages is a primary function. Communication with people around us in personal or professional capacity so as not to confuse them or hurt them with our words is a crucial tact of communication. Most of the times,

our goals can be achieved by not ruffling others with the wrong choice of words, tone and tenor. People generally have a tendency to help each other unless and until rubbed in the wrong way.

42. Keeping ourselves safe is the most primitive life skill which has been used from the time immemorial. It is our natural instinct to stay safe. Taking unnecessary risks and not taking necessary precautions puts us in dangerous situations. Considering difficult and unpredictable political and social conditions, we should be aware of our surroundings all the time. Staying alert does not cost too much but penalty for being unaware of our situation can be very heavy in terms of financial or personal loss.

43. Standard Operating Procedure in case of Emergency needs to be learned and updated every now and then. When disasters or calamities happen, people typically lose their capacity of rational thinking. Their first preference is to get out of the situation. Most of the times, if emergency procedures are not followed, the possibility of damage increases manifold. Keeping people ready for emergencies by practicing emergency evacuations and basic training can help us save a lot of resources in terms of money, time and human lives.

44. Understanding of the basic First Aid is a critical life skill. We cannot predict when we may need to use first aid kits or life- saving procedures like CPR and Heimlich maneuver. We can find ourselves in medical emergency situations any time, having knowledge about not panicking under given circumstances can make a big difference in our reactions in those crucial moments. Knowledge of performing CPR (Cardiopulmonary Resuscitation) and Heimlich maneuver in case of choking can save lives.

45. Surviving without technology and electricity is one of the most essential skill in this modern era. We are so dependent

on modern electronic gadgets and devices that imagining life without electricity and technology is almost impossible. Learning to survive without modern gadgets and electricity is easy. Just switch off the mobiles/laptops, get out of air-conditioned houses and get lost in the woods for a day or two. It is a humbling and stress relieving experience. It opens our eyes to the beauty of the nature and we start appreciating life in a new way.

46. Reading a map is a basic life skill. Whenever we are travelling in remote unfamiliar areas, this skill can help us navigate to our destination safely. We cannot use GPS systems and smartphones at all the locations owing to signal connectivity and availability issues. Using maps and understanding their utility is certainly a skill which we must learn and practice.

47. Ability to fix a flat tire of our car is a god given gift. It saves a lot of time, money and headache. We may have roadside assistance from our car Insurance Company but fixing a flat tire ourselves without waiting for any help can save a lot of money and time. Besides we can always get the flat tire fixed at the next servicing station. Having basic idea about car functions and repairs also helps a lot when we are driving alone on roads where help is miles away.

48. Our ability to go through user reviews and product catalogues of various companies can help us save a lot of time and money while making a major purchase like car or house. We can compare features, specifications, prices, offers etc and make informed decision.

49. Bargaining or negotiation is difficult skill to master. Most of us shy away from negotiations. Being comfortable with asking for a better deal will save us money. Even at our workplaces, we have to negotiate for salary hikes.

50. Accepting criticism and compliments gracefully is an art. Both of these can be flattering and devastating at the same time. Accepting criticism as a feedback to be worked upon and accepting compliments without letting it go to our heads are the best ways of graciously accepting them.

51. Continuously learning about new things which can help us in solving our day to day issues and improving our decision making and productivity.

52. Being actively present while interacting with other people means giving undivided attention to what the other person is saying, listening to understand instead of listening to respond. Asking relevant questions to understand the message in a better way without interrupting. Modern gadgets and devices are constantly distracting us from focusing on anything. We should be careful about using mobile phones and other gadgets while interacting with other people face to face.

53. S.M.A.R.T. Self-Monitoring and Review Techniques was part of our engineering syllabus. It was related to production methodology. It can be used in personal evaluation to constantly monitor our progress towards achieving goals.

54. Managing available resources in the most efficient manner helps us in saving a lot of money and time along with optimum utilization of resources. The resources can be financial or material or manpower related. Having complete control on utilization of money, equipment, facilities and available manpower helps us plan and execute projects in a better way.

The new way of learning

It's time to look at some ways and means of learning modern age life skills in the most healthy and enjoyable environment in complete harmony with our hardwired brain learning patterns.

It's extremely sad and surprising but whenever we discuss about our schools and colleges, one very common point surfaces every-time. Our most vivid and cherished memories about our student lives are related to fun, enjoyment, entertaining and engaging teachers who could teach the most difficult subjects or concepts in the most simple manner. Nobody remembers boring, run of the mill lectures which we were completely disengaged with. Those things could just never arouse our interest to get involved.

Our inherent learning tendencies are purely based on Creativity, Collaboration, Communication, Critical thinking and Choice. We cannot learn anything of importance if these conditions are not present in the learning process.

If we can work on a learning process which can educate us about life skills and specific domain knowledge, our disenchantment and disengagement can be converted into inspiration, motivation and complete participation in the life long education. Results can be miraculous.

New wave of learning process can be based on offering choice of subjects, offering uncontrolled creativity, complete freedom to collaborate with others, complete freedom to question everything while learning all these aspects in the most effective and cordial way of communication.

Let us assume that a school is offering courses wherein, there is no need to go to school every-day. There are three (Basic, Primary and Secondary) courses of 4 years each. Student can opt for professional certification courses after completing these 3 courses successfully.

The school is offering 100 odd options of subjects to choose from. Each subject will have three different syllabi for basic, primary and secondary courses. The subjects range from "how to draw a cartoon" to "Commerce" to "Nuclear Medicine". Each subject will have a carefully set syllabus outline and activity details with testing parameters. No marks or grades will be given after assessment. Only areas of improvement will be highlighted and monitored carefully.

Once we choose 10 subjects per year, we can focus on one subject at a time. We will have to complete a limited assignment on this particular subject every week. We need to submit complete report of the assignment in the school every Monday. We can take guidance from parents, teachers and school any time. Once our teachers evaluate our weekly assignment, they will suggest areas of improvement along with assignment for the next week. All these activities will be closely monitored. Student can opt for change of maximum two subjects in the first Basic course. Students can opt for only one subject change in the second primary course. No subjects can be changed in the third course.

This is a very simplistic explanation of a very complex project which is extremely difficult to monitor & execute. This method can be adopted on a larger scale compared to home schooling. It is primarily based on the assumption that parents and teachers will work together on helping the child get proper education. Most of the physical and mental stress of daily commute and unnecessary focus on subjects of zero interest can be avoided. The free time can be better utilized to learn additional skills or for pursuing hobbies and improving relationships by spending time with friends and family.

Some assumptions are very tricky in this case. First assumption is about the financial viability of the project. How are we going to make sure that the cost of the infrastructure and resources is being taken care of? The second assumption is about the parents' willingness to take responsibility of assuming a crucial role in the learning process of their ward.

Unfortunately some parents are using schools as means of keeping the child away from house and to free themselves of their continuous badgering. I am sure nobody will accept it, but that's ok.

On the similar lines, some parents are opting for home schooling for a long time. 14 of US presidents including Thomas Jefferson and Abraham Lincoln were home schooled. Albert Einstein, Thomas Alva Edison, Honda are some of the notable examples of home schooling. Home schooling is basically about teaching children in our home instead of sending them to schools.

Home schooling is gaining more acceptance due to various reasons. Biggest reason is constantly degrading quality of education in the public or private schools. Second biggest reason is ever increasing cost of schooling. Third reason is "One Size Fits All" solution to all the students. Individual needs and interests are summarily ignored.

Main apprehensions people have about home schooling is about socialization needs of the home schooled children. This can be taken care of by enrolling child to various hobby classes or sports and social activities.

Advantages of home schooling are huge. Many of the prominent professional colleges prefer home schooled students for their course admissions. Most of the countries allow and encourage home schooling. It helps child learn in a better way by interacting with different age groups in the family and society. Huge amount of time can be saved.

Outdated Industrial batch manufacturing education system can be replaced with customized product design and delivery system. Even handcrafted product manufacturing can also be used if we have sufficient resources of time and money with a lot of patience. But in handcrafted production, we can be sure of a meticulously designed and artistically manufactured product of intrinsic art and infinite value, which can last for a lifetime.

Let's start & be ready. Let's not MISS THE BUS!